Mel Bay Presents

Canadian Fiddle Music
Volume One

Compiled by
Dr. Ed Whitcomb

What Is It? — Who Plays It?
444 Original Tunes by 114 Composers

Revised 1998

Hornpipes	Reels	Breakdowns
Strathspeys	Clogs	Schottisches
Polkas	Two-Steps	Marches
Waltzes	Jigs	Rags
Calypsos	Airs	Laments

1 2 3 4 5 6 7 8 9 0

D1552290

Visit us on the Web at http://www.melbay.com — E-mail us at email@melbay.com

This book is dedicated to my mother, Edna,
who taught me to love music
and to my wife, Kai, who shares that love.

Published by Dr. Ed Whitcomb

Canadian Cataloguing in Publication Data

Whitcomb, Edward A.
    Canadian fiddle music
    Includes Bibliographical references
    ISBN 0-9694667-0-6
    1. Fiddle tunes – Canada. 2. Fiddlers –
    Canada – Biography. 3. Fiddling.
    I. Title.

    M40. W34 1990 787.2 C 90-090368-6

Table of Contents

Preface

Between 1987 and 1990 over 200 Canadian fiddlers and lovers of fiddle music helped produce "Canadian Fiddle Music Volume 1". One hundred and twenty of them helped by sharing their fiddle music for free. Countless others spent time in endless conversations with me, sending information, and helping with preparation of the book. Some were paid for specific work such as transcribing or proof-reading, but most helped because they shared the goals of the book.

Those goals were to collect much of the recently-composed Canadian music that was being played here and there, get it professionally prepared, published at a moderate price, and available from coast-to-coast. That would preserve the music, popularize it, make the composers better known, and generally encourage the most important form of folk music in Canada and in Canadian history. The book had several other goals - to broaden knowledge of the violin and the origins and development of fiddle music and its place in Canadian society, to encourage note-reading and chording, to be a book of reference, to teach a bit of Canadian history, culture and geography, and serve as a tribute to many great fiddlers.

We had no idea whether the book would be a success. It was published in June, 1990, and went on sale at the Stratford, Ontario, fiddle contest. By midnight 50 copies had been sold, and we knew that the book was a success. In fact, it has succeeded in every one of its goals. At those first few competitions teenagers were buying it. A year later they were playing those tunes in competitions. They have since been composing their own tunes and sending them to me.

Around two years ago stocks of Volume I began to run down. I suggested to Canadian composers that we do a "revised" edition, and re-publish maybe 200 of the best tunes from Volume I plus around 200 new tunes. Several people said it was a terrible idea - that Volume I was a unique collection of music, and in one's words "should never be out of print". They also advised me to try to find a professional publisher and distributor. So I

sent the book to Mel Bay, one of the biggest and best publishers of folk music in the world. (Mel Bay has published over 60 books of fiddle music alone). They agreed to publish it. One hundred and fourteen composers gave permission to re-publish their music, six others preferred that their music not be published or could not be contacted. A number of corrections have been made to the tunes; the rest of the book is the same.

The idea of calling the fiddle book "Volume I" originated one night when the Schryer triplets were proof-reading tunes. It was close to the cut-off date for publication and over a dozen composers who were expected to submit tunes had not yet done so. I was extremely frustrated, and could imagine getting dozens of great tunes in the mail a week after the book came out. One of the Schryers said something like: "Don't worry, why not call this one Volume I and put all the other tunes in Volume II?"

So the book came out with "Volume I" printed on the title page. Ever since, dozens of people have asked: "Where is Volume II? When is it coming out?" And dozens of fiddlers have sent music for publication if there is a Volume II. So the decision has been taken to do a second volume of Canadian fiddle music, and to do it for all the same reasons that volume I was produced. If you have composed tunes, if you know people who have, then lets get all this Canadian music published and available and, most importantly, played and enjoyed.

My thanks to the 200 or so lovers of Canadian fiddle music who helped with Volume I, to the dozens of people who have supported and sold Volume I and encouraged me to do a second volume. Of all the compliments the book has earned the best, I think, is from a young teenager who said he had worn the covers off the book! Finally, my thanks to "our" new publisher, Mel Bay.

Ed Whitcomb. October, 1998.
Permanent address:
2130 Dutton Crescent,
Ottawa, K1J 6K4.

Acknowledgments

The first acknowledgment is to the 114 composers who have agreed to share their music without compensation because they believe in promoting Canada's musical heritage. The second is to the fiddlers and lovers of fiddle music who support this music and make books like this possible. Two men had considered producing a book like this, Gordie Carnahan and Bill Guest. When they heard this book was underway they offered advice, sent lists of names and addresses, provided music they had collected, obtained signed permission slips from local composers, and transcribed and proofread music. Without them and a Canada Council Grant this project would have died, and the grant was based on letters of support from Anne Lederman, (M.A. thesis on Manitoban Métis Fiddle Music), Elaine Keillor (Professor of Music, Carleton University), and Bill Smith (Professor of Canadian History, University of Manitoba).

A number of people played key roles in making this project possible. Ivan Hicks, Malcolm Dewar, Roma McMillan and Sandy Saundry provided support from the beginning. Anne Lederman, Carmelle Bégin, Lise Ornstein, Kate Kunlay, Dorthy Hogan and David Greenberg provided expert advice – they all have university degrees in music.

The information on fiddling is drawn from a wide variety of sources, but several sections are based on one or two books or articles. The authors whose work is being summarized are identified at the end of each section and in the bibliography.

Encouragement came from dozens of fiddlers. One example is the late Johnny Durocher who told me I could add his name to the then short list of composers who would send music, a key breakthrough for collecting music. Vivian Williams of Voyager Publications generously granted permission to reprint Canadian music from several books.

Music was transcribed and proofread – never for good money and often for free – by Gordie Carnahan, Bill Guest, Gerry Pizzariello, Wilf Gillis, Pierre, Dan and Louis Schryer, Nathan Curry and Web Acheson. The above-mentioned people are responsible for the book being as good as it is; I alone am responsible for the gaps and errors that exist.

Several institutions helped: Carmelle Bégin and the Museum of Civilization, the staff of the National Library, and Larry Delany and Country Music News. The Ottawa Traditional Fiddling and Folk Art Society made a valiant effort to obtain financial support. Special thanks go to Clifford Ford, Executive Director of the Canadian Heritage Music Society, who did the engraving and lay-out. Finally and most importantly, this project would not have been possible without financial support from the Explorations Program of the Canada Council.

Fiddle Music
What it is, where it came from

The origins of fiddle music are not well known. It developed long before music was written down so no one knows exactly what people played centuries ago. We do not know who brought the first fiddle to Canada, when, what they played, or how popular the music was. The history of fiddling in Canada has not been thoroughly researched so there are huge gaps in our knowledge. This essay attempts to summarize some of the literature and scholarship on the subject, but it is in no way itself a work of scholarship, and a number of myths might have survived the editing. Nevertheless the broad outline of our fiddling culture is fairly clear, and amateur enthusiasts of fiddling (like me!) might find this interesting. If it wets some appetites, the bibliography lists numerous books and articles on our fiddling traditions.

Violins, Fiddles, Bows and Music

People have played stringed instruments since ancient times. It takes little imagination to stretch out a cord, twang on it to get a noise, and figure out that if you tighten it you will get a higher note. By Medieval times (1000 to 1500) a variety of musical instruments had been developed to a reasonable degree of sophistication and they were played from the Middle East (where they may have originated) to the Orient, and finally in Europe. Stringed instruments played with a bow gradually gained in popularity: some did not use frets which provided a higher degree of accuracy, and the bow provided continuous sound. The interaction of fingering and bowing techniques created a wide range of possibilities for ornamentation and variety.

The violin or fiddle (they are two words for the same instrument) was developed by Andrea Amati, in Cremona, Italy, sometime around 1550. As a professional musical instrument maker he knew there was a need for something else, so he designed the violin. Sometime after 1600 Stradivari learned how to make them and did a better job of it. His violins are still regarded as amongst the best ever made.

The basic shape of the violin has hardly changed since the days of Amati and Stradivari. It contains almost 100 parts, 4 or 5 different types of wood, various glues and varnishes. It has a flat resonating box, curved top and back, f-shaped sound holes, unfretted fingerboard, and 4 strings (G, D, A and E). The dimensions follow the laws of physics and acoustics, almost perfectly in the hands of a master craftsman.

The secrets of construction seem to lie in some mystical "feel" that the craftsman develops for the wood he is working with: how to cut it, how to shape it, how thick or thin, where precisely to put the sound post and the base bar. The curvature is important: high on the back tends to produce a sweet and soft tone, flat equals strong and robust. The shape of the f holes can vary. An excellent violin is the meeting point of art and science, the craftsman and his creation.

The bow evolved possibly from a weapon of war, the archer's bow. By 1800 a Frenchman, François Tourte, was famous for his bows. He worked out the measurements and balance that are still followed, that is the relationship between the length (73 cm), the increasing width from tip to frog, the balance point (19 cm from the frog or the device that tightens the hairs), and the number of hairs. Smaller bows are of course used, as are smaller violins for children.

Fiddle and violins are the same instrument, but the two terms often refer to the different types of music played on them. When a musician is playing classical or Western Art music, he is using a violin. If he changes style to play jigs or reels, he is then playing a fiddle, but some fiddlers call their instrument a violin. Neither type of music is "better" or "more sophisticated" than the other; both types contain music of great beauty and both types contain music of rather questionable quality. The relative quality of music is really in the ear and mind and cultural background of the listener or player.

Fiddle Music in Europe

In Canada, fiddle music includes jigs, reels, hornpipes, waltzes, polkas, two-steps, strathspeys, schottisches, airs, marches and several other types of music. It is the result of centuries of evolution in Europe and North America. The Americans helped evolve a type of reel called the breakdown and one popular tune (Over the Waves) was written in Mexico. Fiddle music continues to evolve today, and this book includes new types such as rags and stomps and some tunes defined by the composers as "way out".

The main source of this tradition is clearly Europe. No one knows how or when it developed or spread. Since musical literacy developed only slowly, it is difficult to know exactly what types of music were played in Ireland or France or Germany or Norway in 1500 or 1600.

There are references to people dancing a jig or a reel in the sixteenth century but we can not automatically assume that this music was what is understood today as a jig or a reel.

Fiddle music was brought to Canada by successive waves of immigrants. They included the French, English, Irish, Scots, Germans, Scandinavians, Central and Southern Europeans, Eastern Europeans and Americans. It is commonly and probably correctly assumed that the largest source of Canada's fiddle traditions is Celtic (Scottish and Irish), but the other traditions are all important and have had an influence. These influences vary from region to region in Canada. While they intermingle, it is useful to describe some elements of these traditions, how they came to Canada, and how they evolved into Canada's fiddling tradition.

Scottish Fiddling

It took over a century for the fiddle to get to Scotland from Italy, and the route was largely political. When the Kings of France married Italian princesses, the latter brought their musicians to Paris where they introduced the violin. The Kings of France were also related to the Kings of England, and when the English executed Charles I in 1642 his son went to live at the court of the King of France. When Charles II was restored to the throne of England (1660) he brought with him his French wife and her musicians, who played violin, and by around 1670 they had introduced the fiddle to Scotland.

Within a generation it had become one of the dominant music instruments throughout Scotland, spreading gradually from Edinburgh to the Highlands and the islands, eventually to the Hebrides. The professional musicians from King Charles' court taught the local musicians note reading which was essential for playing European Art music. They began writing down the traditional tunes that they played. They began adding techniques from their formal training to traditional music and applying some of the traditional forms to the music flowing from the Continent. What is particularly important is that in eighteenth-century Scotland musicians played both styles or types of music.

Politics had brought the fiddle to Scotland and politics helped make fiddle music dominant in Scottish musical traditions. In 1700, Scotland was an independent country which shared its King with England but had its own government. For a variety of reasons, England decided to conquer all of the British Isles and govern them from London.

Once the Scots accepted political and military defeat they seemed to take a more active interest in developing their distinct musical heritage. To preserve the music and meet a demand for music they had to write it down, and mass-produced books began to appear in the early 1700s. To promote it, they had to develop note-reading, and musical literacy began spreading outwards from Edinburgh. To perfect it they studied in Europe, absorbed the latest techniques and types of music and introduced them to traditional music. By 1760, Scotland had entered the Golden Age of Fiddling. The group of musicians who achieved this were professionals. They studied in Europe and belonged to the Edinburgh Music Club. They played sonatas and minuets in concerts, churches and salons; they also played jigs, reels and strathspeys for dancing.

They succeeded partly because the Scottish aristocracy shared their goals and gave them the political, social and financial support that was needed. The Duke of Gordon hired one of the greatest, William Marshall. The Dukes of Atholl hired the famous family of musicians, Neil Gow and his four sons, especially Nathaniel. These musicians produced numerous books still used today. They wrote out much of the traditional repertoire and added thousands of tunes to it. The fame of Scottish music and the joy of Scottish country dancing spread to the Continent and to the New World and is now enjoyed around the world, specifically in the branches of the Royal Scottish Dance societies.

In the late eighteenth century, a rather odd influence came back from the Continent. In France, a group of writers and philosophers decided that modern society should get back to nature, the simple life and peasant values. The movement was the Enlightenment and Jean Jacques Rousseau was its leading exponent. This philosophy led people to believe that traditional music was better than recently composed original music.

The movement was so strong that some Celtic composers began publishing their tunes as traditional, without putting their names on them. By this time, much of the music being played had been written in the previous generations by middle-class composers employed by nobles; it has been passed down to the present as traditional music written by illiterate peasants with the implication for some that it is "inferior"!

The achievement of the Scottish Golden Age of Fiddling must also be seen in the context of the obstacles over which it triumphed. The Catholic Church had long viewed popular music as the work of the devil – it encouraged or accompanied drinking, dancing, and other forms of evil. But the Church was unable to suppress such music and the decline of Church authority around 1500 helped permit the development of fiddling.

Then in the sixteenth and seventeenth century the Protestant Churches, especially the Presbyterians in Scotland and the Puritans in England, decided to stamp out fiddling once and for all. One could be excommunicated for holding a dance. Fiddles were collected and burned. Town councils passed laws against noise, imposed curfews and specifically banned fiddle music. Those essentially middle-class Scots who listened and obeyed missed out on a few centuries of fun, but the peasants and nobles simply ignored both Catholic and Protestant leaders. The English Government contributed accidentally to the preservation of fiddling. The bagpipes were a Scottish instrument of war, used to instill courage, ésprit-de-corps and clan unity as well as to frighten the enemy. England banned them after the Battle of Culloden (1746) and the pipers took up the fiddle. Bagpipe music has had an enormous influence on fiddling (see Bibliography, Emmerson, Johnson).

Irish Fiddling

Life in Ireland has often been hard, economically, culturally and politically and folk music was enjoyed at fairs, weddings, wakes, market day, relaxation after the day's work, and parties with neighbors and relatives. But the Irish aristocracy does not seem to have supported it as the Scottish nobles did. English nobles with somewhat different culture gradually replaced the Irish, creating a cultural difference between the rich and the poor that did not exist in Scotland. This reinforced the gulf between popular music and the music of the rich and well bred. As the latter became more English, the Irish naturally placed more emphasis on their cultural roots including music to distinguish themselves from their oppressors.

The fiddle came to Ireland in the eighteenth century. The foreign dances with which it was then associated - country dancing and minuets - came as well, and were accepted by people of the class. The fiddle gradually became the main instrument of folk music with home-made fiddles, few middle-class teachers, and little note-reading. The music remained marvelously rich, highly individualistic, varied, innovative and inventive. In the twentieth century, Irish fiddling blossomed, producing musicians like Michael Coleman, regarded by some as one of the greatest fiddlers ever. Many of the styles and varieties if Irish music survived, and they continue to come to

Canada through contacts, recordings and the determination of many Canadian fiddlers to preserve Irish fiddle traditions (see Bibliography, Feldman).

French Canadian Fiddling

French Canadians probably brought fiddle music from France, but little is known definitely about the origins of this music. It was almost certainly enriched in New France by music learned from Scots, Irish and English visitors to the colony. Fiddle music matched the French Canadians' lively temperament, their love of dancing and of family or neighborhood socializing. The music spread quickly throughout New France and the violin, usually home made, quickly became the main musical instrument in Quebec. As in Scotland, the music was banned by the Roman Catholic Church, condemned in Church services, and all the power and influence of the clergy brought to bear in an unsuccessful attempt to stamp it out.

Unfortunately, we have little information on the development of music in Quebec partly because the Church opposed it, and the clergy kept most of the records and literature. From the complaints of the clergy we do know that it was, to them, a major evil, which proves it was very popular. As in other cultures, it was associated in Quebec with dancing and festivals–weddings, family occasions, Christmas and New Year's and community activities like barn-raising. It was usually played solo, one fiddler replacing another who grew tired. Accompaniment consisted mainly of foot stamping, the spoons, and bones. Different dances were done in various parts of Quebec: stepdancing, reels, the lancers, square dance, round dance and the quadrille. In Quebec, family entertainment took on a special significance, to keep the family together, at home, and ensure teenagers were chaperoned. With farm houses deliberately built close together along a river or road (land was laid out in strips, not squares) it was easy to get the neighbors together and a party could last for days.

This social structure built around the home and the family lasted with little change for several hundred years. In the first half of the twentieth century, Quebec produced some great fiddlers–Joseph Allard, Joseph Bouchard, Isidore Soucy, Fortunat Malouin, Bernard Morin, and Jean Carignan. When their records became available, some younger fiddlers were inspired while others put away their fiddles in despair. Then urbanization began to weaken family unity and the fiddling parties at year's end became less common. New forms of music and dance appealed to the young, and new instruments like the guitar became more popular. By the 1940's dance bands featuring the fiddle were in decline, replaced by swing, dixie and the fox trot played mainly on brass instruments. The decline continued until the folk revival of the 1960's and 1970's when groups were formed such as the "Association Québecois des Loisirs Folkloriques" with its twelve regional branches.

These groups, with the support of radio and TV, helped make the traditional fiddlers like Louis "Pitou" Boudreault from Chicoutimi famous. They organized contests and festivals, workshops, magazines to publish music and information, and they supported scholarly research. As in the rest of Canada, other traditions have come and been absorbed–more Scottish and Irish music, English-Canadian music, American influences, and the guitar is often used for accompaniment.

The career of Jean Carignan tells us much about fiddling in Quebec. He began learning the fiddle from his father when he was four (1920). He was soon playing in the streets, in barbershops, at pilgrimage sites, and he earned more on some days than his father. At 10 he met Joseph Allard as well as one of the best step dancers, Jean-Louis Aquin. Carignan could dance, one of the reasons his rhythm was excellent.

At 14 he joined one of the most famous of all Canadian dance bands, George Wade and the Cornhuskers, travelling all over Canada. From 1937 to 1947, he played at Salle St-André in Montreal, to weekend crowds of over 1,000, always as a part-time job (he was a shoemaker and later a taxi driver). He toured in Europe, played his cheap fiddle in Carnegie Hall, New York, and ultimately won the Order of Canada and an honorary doctorate from McGill. He also joined Yehudi Menuhin for "The Music of Man" series on TV.

It is difficult to know the secret of a man like Carignan but it may be that he combined his cultural traditions and great natural ability with a self-taught understanding of classical violin and the techniques of the masters. He went to classical concerts, sat in the front row, and studied the way the violinists played. He would listen for hours to records by fiddlers like Michael Coleman until he had figured out and memorized the notes (fingering) and wrist action (bowing). Then, after he knew in his mind exactly what both hands must do, he would play. Naturally he had his preferences:–he played Irish, Scottish and French Canadian (see Bibliography, Bégin, Ornstein).

Métis Fiddling

One of the most distinctive forms of Canadian fiddling is that of the Métis. In the 18th century the prairies and the North-west Territories were explored by two groups of Europeans. Fur traders from New France crossed the plains, some took Indian wives, and the Métis nation was born. Fur traders from the Hudson's Bay Company, mainly Scottish, also criss-crossed the territories to the Arctic and the Pacific though they did not find a distinctive group like the Métis.

Both groups brought their fiddlers and music and the Métis and Indians adopted it. There are references to fiddlers at Moose Factory on Hudson Bay as early as 1749 and the fiddle was played by Indians at Red River by the early 19th century. The musical culture of the Métis appears to be an amalgamation of the three main influences. The French influence is evident, for example, in a form of stepdancing that evolved, known as the Red River Jig. The Indian influence is evident in the distinctive dances and dance steps and possibly an irregular rhythm and bowing style. The Scottish influence is obvious in the types of tunes and the dances that have been done for over two centuries. They include jigs and reels, schottisches and strathspeys, quadrilles and stepdances. Later other types of music were absorbed–polkas, two-steps, the Charleston and fox trot, plus country and western.

Accounts of life and events in Western Canada suggest that fiddling was an extremely important element of Indian and Métis culture. The fiddle was the main musical instrument, often home-made, and, as in Quebec, was accompanied by foot stamping or, reflecting Indian influences, a drum. The music was played at major events and at house parties. At the latter the furniture was moved away and the dancing went on into the night, with reels and the Red River Jig seemingly the most popular dances. As elsewhere the tradition has evolved, especially with the introduction of the guitar and country and western, but the Métis style remains one of the most distinctively Canadian of the various forms of fiddle music (see Bibliography, Lederman).

Cape Breton Fiddling

Around 1800, Scottish Highland landlords decided to switch their estates from agricultural production to sheep and wool for the booming textile industry of Great Britain. They no longer needed agricultural workers so they expelled them from their farms. Thousands migrated to the New World, settling in New Brunswick, Prince Edward Island and Nova Scotia as well as in Cape Breton Island. In Cape Breton, 30,000 Highlanders constituted the overwhelming majority and their culture dominated. Fiddle music was central to that culture.

As noted above, Scottish fiddle music was undergoing a massive evolution in the eighteenth century, with the successful attempts of the Edinburgh Music Club to marry the old traditional music to a new literate, European-influenced style. This music of the Golden Age gradually spread out from Edinburgh to the Lowlands but it took decades to penetrate the Highlands and northern islands. Thus it was not the dominant music of the Scots who settled Cape Breton, but they learned it later so it is part of their tradition.

The types of music characteristic of Cape Breton are thus what one might expect to find in Scotland today–strathspeys, reels, jigs, marches, airs and laments–but the style is different and Cape Breton has produced some of Canada's greatest fiddlers such as Winston "Scotty" Fitzgerald. These tunes often accompany dancing, especially stepdancing, but are also excellent for listening, as was the Lowland music of the Golden Age. A unique characteristic of this music is the piano accompaniment which sometimes duplicates and backs up the melody (see Bibliography, Dunlay, MacGillivray).

Prince Edward Island and Messer's Down East Style

Fiddle music came to PEI in 1772 with the first British settlers. By the early 1800's, it had been adopted by the Indians and Acadians and was a popular form of entertainment for socials and annual events. By the late nineteenth century, the fiddler was essential for all social occasions: concerts, weddings, parties, picnics, racing, Christmas, fund-raising or barn-rasing. The fiddle was used for many types of dances: stepdancing, jigs, reels, the schottische, round dances, the quadrille, mazurka and polka. In some areas, especially the Catholic northeast, winter featured a sort of continuous party that moved from house to house, often lasting until dawn. And when men went fishing for months on end the fiddle provided entertainment for the crew.

To be a good fiddler was a mixed blessing. One was always on call and it was hard to refuse a neighbor's request. Fiddlers often had to ride or walk miles to an event, play until everyone else was exhausted, then walk home, tend the farm and look after the family. There was a little money in it, but more likely payment was in rum. This has always been the lot of fiddlers and some acquired a deserved or undeserved reputation as drinkers.

The evangelical churches condemned this life arguing, possibly correctly, that good fiddlers were bad farmers. Some of them believed it and refused to allow their children to play music. Some of Canada's fiddlers had to learn when their fathers were away because their fathers had no intention of allowing the children to grow up to be fiddlers!

Social events featuring fiddling and dancing were one of the main forms of entertainment from the founding of the colony until after World War I. Then fiddling went into a decline, as happened to folk music in general in the industrialized world. Radio brought the world's best into the home and the local fiddlers were embarrassed to play. New forms of music appealed to the young. Dancing declined as a form of socializing, entertainment and recreation. But by a strange coincidence, PEI became the basis of a development that defied the trends and did much to save Canadian fiddling–the Don Messer Show.

The radio had a profound influence on culture, hence on fiddling. It inspired many to learn and to copy the masters, it depressed others into quitting altogether. It destroyed much amateur fiddling and made others famous. In its early stages, radio centered on local stations, locally-owned, aimed at a local audience, but with the potential to reach out to a wide, possibly national audience. CFCY, Charlottetown, had a program of fiddling which it supplemented with the new wave of country music (Wilf Carter) and even newer Western music (Hank Snow). An Island fiddler, George Chappelle, and his Merry Islanders did a show carried from coast-to-coast on CBC. It fell apart in the late 1930's and CFCY needed a replacement.

They found Don Messer. Messer is not universally considered one of Canada's great fiddlers. That did not matter for radio because he was a genius as a performer and organizer. What fate demanded of him was not that he outperform other fiddlers in some contest to decide "excellence" but rather that he organize a good show for Canadian radio. He did it extremely well and it gave him a considerable influence on fiddling.

When Messer came to CFCY and Radio Canada in 1939, fiddle music was in decline because other trends in music were becoming more popular. Messer was an entertainer, and as such he adjusted the music he wanted to play to the music the audience wanted to hear. He created a balance of music that responds to a variety of changing demands, and his show became one of the most popular on radio.

10

The basic audience for his program was obviously fiddle enthusiasts, but the secret of his program was to give the general listeners what they wanted–clear, crisp music with excellent rhythm. Messer met the demand by taking complex music and making it simple. He eliminated a lot of the ornamentation, variety and individualism. More sophisticated audiences wanted a professional product. His band read music, they practiced, started and finished precisely. They were professionals.

People were beginning to enjoy swing and dixie. Messer used a clarinct in his band and he played fox trot, jive and Dixie, with guitar and piano solos for variety. People wanted more than just music; Messer used the best MC's available, and they complemented what he personally lacked–warmth and humor. People wanted nostalgia and seriousness–Marg Osborn and Charlie Chamberlain sang a few of the old songs and a hymn or two. People wanted youth, action and ethnic diversity; Messer provided Ukrainian dancers and young step-dancers. People wanted a good fast toe-tapping beat, and Messer played tunes far faster than normal, but at some cost to expression according to more traditional fiddlers.

His program was loved from coast to coast, by old and young, in cities and farms, in all provinces, and by most ethnic groups. It was not, however, liked by two groups of people. One was the traditionalist fiddler who resented his simplification of style, the destruction of individuality that resulted from radio-TV popularity, and the modernization he provided. The other was the cultural élite who controlled the CBC and viewed fiddling as an inferior form of music. To the amazement of Canadians the show was cancelled at a time when it was one of two Canadian programs rated in the top ten.

Oddly the cancellation had a positive effect on fiddling. It shocked a number of people into realizing how vulnerable Canadian folk culture was. What would happen when Don Messer passed on? Messer went on a cross-Canada tour. The timing coincided with Centennial year and dozens of communities organized fiddle competitions as part of the celebrations. A movement developed to save and promote fiddle music.

Messer continued to play on many more TV shows and to tour extensively. His music books were probably the most popular in Canada and are still for sale. The style he and others developed became known as Down East, characterized by waltzes, jigs, polkas and reels, played simply and with excellent dance rhythm and it had enormous influence, especially in Ontario and the West. It is called by some the "Canadian style".

Don Messer was not replaced on CFCY when he left for Halifax in 1956 partly because radio-TV stations were rapidly replacing local shows with imported national or international programs. In 1977 the PEI Fiddlers' Association was founded by Bishop Faber MacDonald. It was modelled after the newly founded Cape Breton Fiddlers' Association. It emphasize Scottish-Cape Breton music. Fiddlers learned from printed music, and played in groups. The Association has been enormously successful in encouraging younger fiddlers, improving repertoire and techniques and bringing back the music of the early 1900's. The summer tourist is bound to hear this music at picnics and lobster suppers throughout the Island (see Bibliography, Hornby, Sellick).

Fiddling in Ontario and the West

East of the Ottawa River, Canada has three fairly distinct styles of fiddling: French Canadian, Cape Breton and Down East, with dozens of variations within them. West of the Ottawa River there is no dominant style. There are instead a number of areas where one of the above styles is dominant and, overall, a sort of "melting pot" of all these styles plus American and other foreign influences. The fiddling culture reflects, of course, the types of immigrants who settled these provinces.

Not all Highland Scots went to Cape Breton and the Maritimes. A large group settled in Glengarry County about 80 miles southeast of Ottawa. They brought the same music and they formed a sufficiently cohesive and strong community to preserve it. Throughout the 19th century French Canadians spread across the Ottawa River and developed French communities across Ontario and the West along Lake Huron, in the Clay Belt of Nothern Ontario, in St. Boniface, and in towns in southern Saskatchewan and central Alberta. They took their music with them and they preserved it.

The largest group to settle Ontario in the nineteenth century was Irish Protestant. These people often played or knew fiddle music, but it was not so strong a tradition with them partly because the Presbyterian church was opposed to dancing, fiddling and partying. They were joined especially in the mid-nineteenth century by Irish Catholics who settled both sides of the Ottawa River (and the Saint John River in New Brunswick and many of the Newfoundland outports). These people loved the fiddle. They brought their music, retained it, developed it, and it has become one of the dominant strands in Ontario's fiddle tradition. At the same time, there was a steady migration from the Maritimes to Ontario, especially south and southwest Ontario. These Maritimers were joined by immigrants coming directly from Scotland, Ireland, England and the USA. All these people brought their styles of fiddle music producing a different mix of styles in the Toronto to Windsor area than one would hear in eastern Ontario, Quebec or the Maritimes.

Economic activity had a profound influence on fiddling in Ontario and elsewhere in Canada. Canada's most important export was timber, and logging camps were developed in all the major river valleys and all along the fringe of agricultural land. Laborers and farmers would spend the winter months in these camps, and the best form of entertainment and relaxation after a day of cutting trees was fiddling and stepdancing. This ensured that a fairly large portion of the adult male population knew fiddle music and large numbers of them played it. Fiddle music was not just the overwhelming element in their musical culture, it was the heart of their entire cultural and social lives.

Manitoba was settled in the late 19th and early 20th centuries, mainly from southern Ontario, and this predominantly British population spread across the prairie provinces into B.C. It was joined by steady immigration from the Maritimes and the United States, all these strains reinforcing the type of "melting pot" fiddle tradition emerging in southwest Ontario. At the same time, a different wave of immigration was arriving from northern, central and eastern Europe–Norwegians, Swedes, Germans, Poles, Ukrainians and Russians, settling north of the "Anglo-Saxon belt".

The Norwegians and Swedes had a well-developed fiddle tradition and they easily assimilated the trends of Canadian fiddle music. The Germans brought their love of the waltz and polka. (Don Messer is of German background.) The Poles and Ukrainians brought and retained their own music, instruments and dances, and made a great contribution to Canadian fiddling. Their polka is done with a speed and vigor not found in other Canadian cultures.

One social activity became particularly important in Western Canada though it was popular everywhere in English-Canada: the Friday-night dance in the school house. Western Canada has a far harsher climate and more difficult environment than Eastern Canada. The sense of bleakness and isolation was reinforced by the nature of land settlement, which produced great distance between farms. Settlement by a variety of ethnic groups, many of whom did not speak the same language, further fragmented society.

One of the most important ways of getting the whole

community together on the prairies became the Friday-night dances in the local, one-room school house. Entire families came to visit and dance, women bringing the food, the children playing or attempting to dance until they fell asleep. The schoolteacher (young, single, often from Ontario, and looking for a husband?) often provided piano accompaniment, and a variety of fiddlers took turns with the music. The combination of dances was slightly different from those of Ontario, quite different from Quebec and the Maritimes, with more square dances, waltzes, polkas, schottisches, two-steps and slow (modern) waltzes. The men would slip outside to discuss crops and politics and have a nip of cheer, often home made.

This was probably the most popular form of entertainment and socializing in the prairies until after World War II. Then the combined effects of twentieth-century technology took their toll. Urbanization and farm consolidation reduced the number of farms and increased the distance between them. Radio and TV made home entertainment more popular than group fun. Cars carried the families to town to watch movies. Other forms and styles of music became popular–the guitar, rock and roll. Music became passive, listening to professionals instead of dancing to the local amateurs.

As in other parts of Canada, this decline continued until the 1960's, when the folk music revival set in. A group formed the Swift Current Old Time Fiddlers Association and a similar organization sprang up in Maple Creek. Their records captured the music of the one-room school houses. An immediate effect was that children and teenagers decided that fiddling was fun and began to learn. Today there are no one-room school houses in Western Canada. There are over two dozen annual fiddle competitions. The BC Fiddlers Association alone has 12 regional branches. All are devoted to preserving a main form of Canada's music heritage, fiddling (see Bibliography, Newlove, Proctor).

Fiddle Competitions

Fiddle competitions are probably about as old as fiddling. That is because it is natural for people to discuss who the best fiddler is, argue about it, get the fiddlers to play, and get together to have some fun and cheer the fiddlers on. Human beings are competitive–in military skills, in athletics, in cooking, in music. It would take no time to realize that one needed a judge respected by the players plus some rules. Stepdancing, which goes hand-in-hand with fiddling, has long been a competitive sport, one test being who could dance the longest.

We do not know when they originated or how they evolved, but there have been contests in Scotland for centuries. There are references to fiddle contests in the United States as early as 1736, and we can assume they have long existed in Canada. The coming of cars and better roads in the early twentieth century expanded them. Some of the earliest evidence of competitions dates from 1926 when Joseph Allard of Quebec won a competition in Maine, giving his career a huge boost. In the same year fiddlers in PEI decided to hold a contest in Charlottetown with first prize a ticket to a major contest in Boston. Forty contenders showed up and it took two days to select the winner, Neil Cheverie. He then placed third in Boston, and the best stepdancer, Robert Weeks, placed first. The organization and success of the Charlottetown contest and the victories in Boston had considerable influence on fiddling and contests in the Maritimes. (Those contests were a part of a nation-wide movement in the USA sponsored by Henry Ford. He was a great supporter of old-time music and piped fiddle music into his car dealerships.)

As the popularity of fiddling declined in the early twentieth century, so did the popularity of contests. By 1960, they were few and far between. Amongst the survivors of that era is Shelburne, which began in 1951 to raise money for the Rotary Club and the Maritime Open, which began in 1950. Then in the early 1960's fiddling came back in style, and with it the contests.

In Swift Current a number of people felt it shameful that fewer and fewer people played the fiddle. In 1965 a group of concerned citizens organized a contest which was an enormous success. It has been going ever since. In Pembroke and Bobcaygeon contests began, now over 20 years old. In Cape Breton a TV show "The Vanishing Fiddler" alerted people to the imminent death of fiddling. They got out their fiddles, called the neighbors and began playing. In 1973 they organized a massive rally in Glendale where thousands gather every summer to play and listen.

Today there are over 100 annual contest or jamborees across Canada: a dozen in B.C., 10 in Saskatchewan, countless ones in Quebec where hotel owners organize them. No other musical instrument attracts this type of attention or has created this type of spontaneous organization. Prizes are sponsored by companies, but unlike many other types of cultural activities governments do not support fiddling, our national form of musical culture.

Contests vary greatly but there are a number of common characteristics. Most are held in the summer, the main ones lasting two days. They usually include stepdancing which is a crowd pleaser because it combines music with dance, as fiddle music was designed, and it offers color, variety, noise, activity and beauty. A variety of fiddle classes have evolved: under 12, under 18, over 60, intermediate, champion, with all sorts of variations. In Quebec the intermediate class is often divided into A and AA giving the less skilled a chance to compete with their peers. Sometimes in Quebec all adults compete in a single class the fist night, and the results of that determine who is in what class.

In some contests there is a woman's class but this practice seems to have declined, possibly because women are as good as men though fewer play the fiddle. Novelty fiddling is a spectator sport: people play fiddle tunes on saws and beer bottles, play while standing on their heads, fiddle and stepdance simultaneously, play duets with bows on each others' fiddles, and so on. Duet or Twin fiddling is not well defined: often two fiddlers simply play the same tune together but one does hear some perfect harmony. A relatively new class is gospel with anything from a jazzed up "Old Rugged Cross" to hymns that bring tears to the eye.

A complex set of rules has evolved, again with lots of variations. Contestants are allowed three to four minutes and may or may not be penalized for going over the limit. Contestants are allowed one form of accompaniment–most choose a piano but some use a guitar or play solo. Three tunes are usually played: a waltz (3/4), a jig (6/8), and a reel (2/4 or 4/4), but the under 8 class can play anything. This use of waltz, jig and reel seems to have originated in Shelburne and may reflect the influence of Messer's Down East style and square dancing. It is up to the judges whether one is disqualified for playing a polka instead of a reel.

Rules often say that the tunes must be "old time". That is not defined–it may mean Down East rather than Scottish or Irish; it may mean music that is more clearly designed for dancing than for listening. It normally excludes music influenced by classical or jazz plus "novelty" fiddling as in "Listen to the Mocking Bird". In some contests one must play different tunes in the finals. In some areas if you win in intermediate you have to move up to the open class and if you win that you may have to retire for a year or so. That means the best cannot always compete but more have a chance. Some technical rules have had to be adopted, for example if a string breaks.

There is a great deal of gentlemanly conduct and intelligent interpretation of the rules. If an 85 year old

13

plays the tunes in the wrong order and dwells a bit on his favorite waltz few will complain, and people who have won often simply stop entering so others can have a chance. One often sees a champion-class fiddler accompanying another fiddler who is in the same class, encouraging him to do his best.

There are similar classes and rules for stepdancing. Contestants usually dance consecutively a clog (2/4), a jig (6/8), and a reel (2/4 or 4/4) with the second half of the reel in very fast time, i.e. a breakdown. Under 12 and over 50 can usually dance anything. Group dancing is unique because the dancers can put together a show with combinations of individual and group dancing, themes, acrobatics, parents and children, boys and girls, anything to amuse the audience and impress the judges. Stepdancing is particularly popular in Ontario. It is heavily influenced by the Irish of the Ottawa Valley and was kept alive by the late Donnie Gilchrist. In the West and North one does jigging, (clogging), a dance derived from Quebec with Irish, Indian and Métis influences.

Judging is, of course, controversial. There are usually three and they score each candidate for things like tone, style, accuracy, rhythm and technique. Often in Quebec they are in a separate room and do not hear the players' name or the audience response. Others believe the judges should be in the audience, in front of the stage, to get the full flavor of the performance including how the audience judges it. By their scores the judges define what is meant by "old time". In some contests a classical-style fiddler cannot likely win because the technique, feeling, style and sound are "wrong"–the same person might be a champion elsewhere. Some contestants could play an incredibly beautiful waltz but if it is no good for waltzing they may not win.

It is an advantage, of course, to be playing in your home town. On the other hand it is heartwarming to see the reaction when Quebec fiddlers win in Ontario and vice-versa. It is an advantage to play, for example, Scottish style if the judges are Scottish–that is a fact, not bias, and a serious competitor takes advantage of these things the same way a sailor takes advantage of the wind. It is nice to see organizers who select one judge who likes Down East style and another who prefers Scottish/Irish, but who is to say what is best? If the people in some area prefer Down East then they should get judges who do too and let them select the best Down East style fiddlers.

The top contestants eventually become a sort of class by themselves. Judges have to be wary before ignoring them in selecting the finalists, which means you have to play a bit better to get into the class than to stay in it. This is true of many activities; it is known as paying your dues. It may not be 100% "fair", but perhaps one should not select champions exclusively on the basis of a three-minute performance. What is amazing is the degree to which the top fiddlers and the audiences as a whole agree with the results.

The contest tradition has been one of the main forces behind the revival of fiddling in Canada. When the first contest was organized in Swift Current, people who had not played in decades brushed up a few tunes, participated, loved it and proposed making it an annual event. That phenomena occurred across Canada in the 1960's. More people started to practice. They formed groups. They learned new tunes. They met more fiddlers. They made records and sold or gave them to each other. They began writing new tunes and playing them in public. Prizes and good judging led to improvements in techniques and the copying of the better performers. The contests created a vast network for sharing information and music, learning techniques, discussing books and records, finding new teachers, and making friends. Young fiddlers in particular met the champs and went home full of new tunes, new ideas and enthusiasm.

The stage at a contest or jamboree is just the tip of the iceberg and only a tiny fraction of the music is made on the stage. One hears the fiddlers in the warm-up room, the hallways, the parking lots and the motels. One can see groups of fiddlers including women playing medleys of reels in the men's washroom and no one seems to mind. As the big contests are two-day summer events hundreds of people brings vans and tents, and the music in "fiddle city" goes on till dawn. Some of these people bring pianos, bass violins, sound systems and whole bands. People drive for a thousand miles to attend and meet friends not seen for a year. Substantial quantities of beer are consumed–no one bothers the drinkers and no one bothers the non-drinkers. Unilingual French play with unilingual English because the language is music.

There are, however, controversial aspects to fiddle contests. The adoption of the waltz-jig-reel format has artificially increased the popularity of those three types of music. The preference for Down East style has similarly increased the popularity of it at the expense of more complicated and varied music. The concentration on tunes that win competitions has narrowed repertoire and in particular has harmed the uniquely individualistic styles of former times, also affected by radio, records and TV. The fiddlers who naturally flourish in competitions become more prestigious and influential than peers whose style may be better. Some of the best fiddlers do not go to contests or will not play in them. Fortunately the styles of fiddling not favored in contests flourish in homes and clubs and on records, and many fiddlers play "contest" and "traditional" styles equally well.

Fiddling in Canada Today

This essay brings us to the state of fiddling in Canada today. We have an instrument, the violin or fiddle, that originated in Italy and became one of the most important instrument for both Western Art music and popular music. It was applied to a form of music that had developed throughout Europe long before the settlement of Canada. The music and the fiddle were brought to Canada over the past four centuries by most of the groups of European immigrants, the French, Irish, Scots, Scandinavians, Germans, East Europeans and Americans.

In Canada some of this music has remained relatively unchanged, but much of it has evolved with the passage of time and the continuous intermingling of styles and traditions. It has prompted Canadians by the hundreds to compose tunes which enrich the world's heritage of popular music. Over 100 Canadians have freely contributed music to this collection. That includes almost every type of fiddle music, composed by Canadians of many ethnic backgrounds, and from all provinces. It includes music one can call traditional such as jigs and reels and strathspeys, plus modern styles such as rags and a few tunes that are "way out". This music was composed over the past half century, up to May, 1990.

Types of Music

A jig's a jig but what's a strathspey?

Most Canadians know what a waltz is. Most fiddlers can tell you what a jig is. Not all fiddlers can explain the difference between a two-step, a polka and a reel but they can usually play all of them correctly. Few fiddlers can explain or play a hornpipe because it is now confused with American hornpipes which are reels.

This essay is designed to explain the types of tunes fiddlers play and the relationship with the dances they are designed to accompany. Some of these types of music overlap because of the way they are played, for example a fast two-step becomes in effect a polka. Attempting to be too precise can be confusing and in fact inaccurate–even the experts do not agree on these terms. Description is not a straight-jacket–fiddlers play music in whatever fashion makes them happy. Here, then is a general description of most types of Canadian fiddle music with the warning that there are many exceptions and differences of opinion and interpretation about these definitions.

The Waltz: The waltz is possibly the most clearly indentifiable of fiddle tunes–it is in 3/4 time and anything in 3/4 time is a waltz. Two types of dance are done to it–the waltz (a couple) and the waltz-clog (stepdance), plus skating, of course. It originated in Austria, became enormously popular throughout Europe in the nineteenth century and Strauss made it acceptable to royalty. But it is not Celtic so it is most popular west of Quebec, certainly not in Cape Breton.

The Jig: The jig is also clearly identifiable–it is almost always in 6/8 time. The origins of the word are debated. In medieval France music was played on an instrument that looked like a leg of lamb, a gigot. In medieval Germany they played an instrument known as the geige, and the Italian had the giag or gige. Jigs are used for step dancing, polkas, Scottish country dancing, and first change in square dancing, but in Quebec "la gigue" refers to all types of music for stepdancing, including reels. As a form of music the jig probably originated in Ireland, perhaps as early as the sixteenth century. There are variations of it: single (6/8), double (6/8), or triple (9/8), also called a hop jig or slip jig. It is immensely popular in all parts of Canada.

Reel: The reel is the most common form of fiddle music. The name probably comes from the English verb "to reel" and after doing a couple of reels or square dances people will stagger. The name could also come from the common figure eight pattern of Scottish country dancing in which one "reels" around. Its origin is probably Scottish, at least as early as the sixteenth century. It is lively and fairly fast (110-130 beats to the minute), in 2/4 or 4/4 time. It is used for the reel, polka, square dance (second or third change) and stepdancing, and is played everywhere in Canada, especially in Quebec.

The Breakdown or Hoedown: Americans made the reel faster, more noisy and vigorous and called it a breakdown, a name that makes a lot of sense. In stepdance competitions one dances, a clog, a jig, and a reel. In fact, the reel is divided in two parts, the second one being faster and with more footwork. What is in fact being played is a clog, a jig, a reel and a breakdown. A hoedown is another American word for breakdown, but also means jamboree.

The Strathspey: In the 18th century executions were a public form of entertainment. The accused was allowed to give a speech or, if musical, to entertain the crowd one last time. When James MacPherson was about to be hanged he allegedly played a slow reel–MacPherson's Rant–and he did it so well that the tempo came to be adopted throughout Scotland. This happened at Strath, in the valley of the Spey. As a slow reel it can have more melodic embellishment but is characterized by a dotted eighth or sixteenth note (ie. a rest instead of a note) known as the Scottish snap. For listening it is played along with a slow then fast reel. The strathspey is a slow dance for four couples but can also be used for stepdancing.

Schottische/Clog: The schottische is in 2/4 time, à couple dance done with three steps and a hop. Clog music is the same tempo but with different accent (on the fourth note) and is used for the (slow) part of stepdancing. "Balkan Hills" or "Road to the Isles" are typical schottisches; "Minstrel's Fancy" is a typical clog. They can both be used to clog, but a clog makes a poor schottische.

The Hornpipe: This is the least understood and most commonly misnamed type of fiddle music. It was named for a northern English instrument wherein the sound of a pipe (reed or fife) was amplified by attaching it to a horn (bugle). In the sixteenth century shepherds amused themselves with it and developed a slow dance for the

music in triple time (6/8). In the 18th century it was changed to 2/4 or 4/4 meter but with the emphasis remaining on the first three beats, especially in the last bar (called pom, pom, pom). As such it is a slow reel, and that is a "proper" hornpipe. But in the mid-19th century the Americans adopted it, speeded it up to breakdown tempo, and that is what most North American hornpipes are now ("Democratic Rage", "President Garfield"). To appreciate the difference one should listen to the "Londonerry Hornpipe" played by Leo Cremo (hornpipe) and Graham Townsend (reel).

The Polka, March and Two-Step: The polka originated in Central Europe, possibly Czechoslovakia, and became immensely popular in the nineteenth century. It came to Canada with the Germans and Slavs, becoming popular west of Ottawa, then in Quebec, but especially in Western Canada. It is in 2/4 tempo, faster than a reel that is being played properly, but usually uses 8 notes to the bar instead of 16 and therefore sounds slower. Like the waltz which came from the same area, it is a couple dance, done in circles, very quickly amongst Ukrainians. The March (eg. "Radetsky's March") is the same tempo, but, with exceptions such as "Under the Double Eagle" is not normally used for dancing. The two-step is a sort of slow polka, danced more like a fox trot. "Maple Sugar" is played as a two-step in Ontario and a polka in Western Canada.

Airs, Laments and Rags: Fiddle music is dance music, but there are exceptions. The air is a haunting melody played slowly and sweetly, sometimes without accompaniment. It can be 2/4, 3/4, or 4/4. A lament is an air with a sad melody, named for a (departed) friend of loved one. At the other end of the scale the Americans applied the fiddle to the early twentieth century music such as ragtime to produce rags, stomps, shuffles, fox trots, and easy-listening country and western. In addition some old traditional forms such as the galope retain popularity in some parts of Canada.

Notes on Tunes, Notes and Chords

Some people will read some of this music and say "It isn't right." Some of them will be right. Some music when written out is not the same as it is when recorded, because the fiddler making the recording may add flourishes or grace notes and variations on the pick up notes or emphasis. Some of this music was transcribed off tapes where the composer played his own tune several different ways. Some of the music submitted clearly contained errors such as missing rests. For consistency endings and

beginnings had to be standardized which makes it appear different from what was submitted. In some cases, after long debate and much playing, agonizing decisions were taken to make a small change or to use music as submitted. Some of these were "judgement calls": different musicians, editors or proof readers could have printed it differently. There is much delicate balancing between the over-riding goal of exactness to the original and some obligation to consistency and accuracy.

One rule we attempted to follow was "keep it simple"– fiddlers can make their own arrangements.

Chords have been added by a variety of people: the composers, the transcribers, the proofreaders, and a number of fiddlers and pianists. This provides a variety of arrangements and styles and should serve as a useful teaching tool for piano-guitar. But chording is very much a matter of personal style, not a matter of "correct" or "incorrect" chords. These chords will be helpful to some, unnecessary to others, and can be altered to suit the fiddler and pianist.

The tunes have all been submitted as original compositions by the composers to be "used with permission" in this book. The composers have copyright on them and they cannot be reproduced or played for profit without the permission of the composer. Every effort has been made to ensure that they are original tunes and that no existing copyright has been violated in reproducing them here.

The Composers

Some composers sent pages of information, clippings and pictures and some sent little or nothing. Information also comes from letters, conversations, record covers, and from books especially Bill Guest's on Canadian fiddlers. Some wanted addresses included and some did not, so it was decided to include city/town only. One call to directory assistance will yield the phone number. This section underlines the tremendous variety of backgrounds of Canada's fiddlers. There is every ethnic group: French, English, Scottish, Irish, Métis, German, American, Scandinavian, Jewish and East European. There is every level of musical knowledge, from fiddlers who do not read music to ones with degrees in music. There is every profession and social class in Canada. There are fiddlers from every province, every age group and both sexes. These are Canada's best, and they are sharing their music for free, for the love of fiddling.

Web Acheson is known throughout Ontario as a judge, contest-fiddler, back-up fiddler, composer, and professional musician (accordion, base, mandolin and guitar). He transcribed some of the music for this book. Bell Ewart, Ontario.

Abbie Andrews is one of many who began with classical violin and switched to fiddle. By the 1930's his band, The Canadian Ranch Boys, were appearing on radio and music was his profession. In 1955, a serious accident ended his playing, but his musical reputation continued to grow because of his dedication to it, and the quality of his compositions. St. Catharines, Ontario.

Bill Andrews took up fiddling at 15 and played with his brother's band, The Canadian Ranch Boys. He played for years in North Bay, including on TV and radio with Irwin Prescott, father of the Prescott Brothers. St. Catharines, Ontario.

John Arcand is a Saskatchewan fiddler who writes reels in the French-Canadian/Western Canadian/Métis style. Big River, Saskatchewan.

Bruce Armitage is typical of the many Irish fiddlers from the Quebec side of the Ottawa River, an area where Irish fiddling can be heard every night in pubs and homes. Quyon, Quebec.

Alfred (Eddy) Arsenault is a fisherman and named his compositions (The Draggers Reel) for his trade, "dragging" in fish. He has made one LP. Egmont Baie, P.E.I.

Dave Bagnell began fiddling at age 6 and has won contests in both classical, old-time and group fiddling. He plays fiddle, violin, sax, clarinet and piano, and has judged contests all over the Maritimes. Don Messer has recorded some of his music. Truro, N.S.

Gerald Bailey began playing fiddle at seven. He played in his own band for 25 years and has continued to play in bands, and to enter and judge contests in southwest Ontario. He has composed over 40 tunes. Sarnia, Ontario.

Myllie Barron is a retired carpenter. He learned music from a correspondence school. After a 25-year gap he returned to fiddling becoming a champion and a judge on the West coast and as far south as Idaho. He has numerous trophies, one LP, and makes violins as a hobby. Salmon Arm, B.C.

Donald Angus Beaton was one of the famous "Beatons of Mabou", Cape Breton. He wrote over 50 tunes and played all his life for concerts, weddings, dances and festivals. His music has been published and recorded by his sons, Kinnon and Joey and in numerous records. Deceased.

Elizabeth Beaton accompanied her husband, Donald, for decades and is one of Cape Breton's many famous pianists.

Kinnon Beaton was born in Mabou in 1956, the son of Donald and Elizabeth, and began fiddling at 12. He has written over 400 tunes. He has entertained audiences from Nova Scotia to Boston, Detroit and Toronto, has published several books of his own and his father's music, and is widely recorded. Port Hawkesbury, N.S.

Mel Bedard is a Métis fiddler who has toured Western Canada, played the contest circuit and made numerous records. Selkirk, Manitoba.

Reg Bouvette was influenced by Andy Dejarlis with whom he played for 10 years. He has made at least five LP's. Winnipeg, Manitoba.

Denis Brisson played in a band with his brothers for almost thirty years. He has won 30 trophies and has written over 30 tunes, some recorded on his own albums. Embrun, Ontario.

Malcolm "Mac" Brogan came from a family of fiddlers and had his own band in the 1950's and 1960's. He has made one LP. Chipman, N.B.

Leo Browne was born in County Tyrone in 1908, trained in classical violin, and brought his Irish fiddling to Canada in 1926. He played for years in Montreal and was influential in the development of Jean Carignan's understanding of Irish music. He is a founding (and life) member of the Ottawa Traditional Fiddling and Folk Art Society. Ottawa.

Lawrence Buckler, learned to play by ear listening to Don Messer on radio. At University (he is a professional engineer) he took lessons in classical violin, even studying the characteristics of the instrument and how it is made. He prints his compositions on a computer. Dartmouth, N. S.

Gordie Carnahan began playing piano and then, at age 18, heard the fiddle and fell in love with it. He has been playing and writing music in Manitoba ever since, including TV appearances and shows and contests all over the Prairies. He became an expert at transcribing music, and when composers learned this they came to his house, worked with him at contests or jamborees, or sent cassettes with the result that he has a collection of some 4000 fiddle tunes. There is absolutely no question that without Gordie Carnahan's support this book would never have been produced. Brandon, Manitoba.

Art Champion learned to play in the 1930's and began competing in the 1970's. Melita, Manitoba.

Jim Chapman has played for dances for decades. The tunes in this book were originally recorded in 1963, and he is now spending more time composing. Moncton, N.B.

Sam Chernecki is from Manitoba.

Norm Cheyne is a self-taught left-handed fiddler who does not change the strings over (right-handed fiddle). Deloraine, Manitoba.

Yvon Cuillerier is a professional musician known throughout Quebec and Ontario as a master of a variety of fiddle styles - French Canadian, Scottish and Irish, and European. He and the pianist Theo Bujould made a number of LP's for Sortileges, a group dedicated to the promotion of French Canada's musical culture. He played in Royal Albert Hall, London, and in Canada Day celebrations on Parliament Hill. St. Leonard, Quebec.

Ken Davidson plays mainly guitar. Dartmouth, N.S.

Carol (Kennedy) Dawson is from Glengarry, the heart of Scottish fiddling in Ontario. She played piano for Johnny Mooring and Graham Townsend and has performed in Nashville, South America, Australia and Europe. She owns a music store in Pembroke, Ontario.

Bill Delorme began playing fiddle at seven. When Don Messer visited, Delorme played on the show, invited Messer to his house and played some of his competitions. Messer recorded and published them. Deceased.

Roddy Dorman learned the fiddle in the 1940's. He led two bands for 25 years doing numerous shows and concerts. He has appeared on Don Messer's Jubilee. He is a contest fiddler, and won the Maritime Open. His tunes are in Don Messer's Anthology and he has made numerous records. Halifax, N.S.

Kate Dunlay began playing violin in school in Boston and discovered traditional music in University. She has since became one of Canada's leading experts and scholars of Cape Breton music and of its Scottish origins (please see the Bibliography). She and her husband, David Greenberg, live in Toronto.

Carl Elliott, like Johnny Mooring, comes from Nova Scotia but spent two decades playing fiddle in Ontario. He has played in bands, produced five square dance LP's, successfully toured the contest circuit and is a judge. He comes from a musical family and his sons also play fiddle and guitar. Economy, N.S.

Bob Emerson lives in Manitoba.

Duncan Emerson lives in Brandon, Manitoba.

Beth Fenton lives in Albert, N.B.

Ivan Fisher is from Grandview, Manitoba.

Ron Gain is a prominent Irish-style fiddler in the Perth area of Ontario, where a strong Scottish fiddling tradition survives. Delta, Ontario.

Wilf Gillis, from Arisaig, Nova Scotia, represents the eighth generation of fiddlers in his family. His grandfather played in a string quartet. Wilf studied violin at the Halifax Conservatory. He has written numerous tunes, made one LP, is a judge, and is an original member of the Cape Breton Symphony. As such he tours regularly in North America and Great Britain. Ottawa.

Paul Gitlitz has a degree in music from the University of British Columbia and has played fiddle, mandolin, banjo and guitar with numerous bands and ethnic groups in British Columbia. He has played and/or danced in schools, festivals, TV shows and been musical director for theatre productions. Richmond, B.C.

David Greenberg began classical violin lessons at age four in Maryland, U.S.A. He won his first competition at age eight. He has studied Western Classical music at University and regularly tours Canada, the U.S.A. and Europe playing classical and baroque with chamber orchestras. That is his profession, but his hobby is, with his wife Kate Dunlay, playing and writing Cape Breton music. Toronto, Ontario.

Bill Guest has a University degree in music, plays a number of string and wind instruments, and has taught music in high school. He has won numerous competitions, played and toured on the Don Messer show, composed over 300 tunes, made records, written a book on Canadian fiddlers, published three books of fiddle music and prepared several others for publication. He is regarded as one of the ablest transcribers of music, and he prepared and checked much of the music for this book. Without his help this book could not have been made. Dartmouth, N.S.

Rufus Guinchard is famous for his unique method of fiddling. He began teaching himself at eleven, looking out a window on his left to ensure no one surprised him. He thus held the fiddle against his right shoulder and held the bow half way up, and has played that way for eighty years! He has played for dances and festivals all his life keeping alive the traditional music of Newfoundland. With the revival of folk music in the 1970's he became justly famous, playing throughout Canada and in France, making records and appearing on numerous TV shows and festivals. Hawkes Bay, Nfld.

Gerald Hamilton began learning fiddle from his father at age 16. He is mainly a dance fiddler but became interested in competitions through group stepdancing. London, Ontario.

Ian Hamilton began playing fiddle at 20, and also plays accordion and trombone. He is a student of Chuck Joyce and has won numerous contests, some in competition with his father, Gerald. London, Ontario.

Jack Hayes represents one of the most important elements in Canadian fiddling. He writes Scottish music designed for Country Dancing. He has been a figure in the Toronto music scene for generations. His music has been recorded by Bobby Brown for Scottish Country Dancing. Toronto.

Brian Hébert began playing at five, has a degree in music and teaches music. He has composed over 30 tunes, made several LP's and won major contests. Pembroke, Ontario.

Dave Hepworth studied violin and learned fiddle from his father. He has won over 45 trophies in the prairie provinces. He began composing to avoid a major problem in contest fiddling, having another contestant play the tune he had practiced. Regina, Saskatchewan.

Ivan Hicks played his first dance at age seven with his father, Curtis, a fiddler. He learned mandolin, piano, and Hawaiian and Spanish guitar, and helped form a band while still a teenager. His band "The Maritime Express" has recorded some of his 10 LP's, and he has won the Maritime Open and been a judge. He has produced a book of fiddle music, and has been inducted into the New Brunswick and North American Musical Halls of Fame. Riverview, N.B.

Lorimer Higgins was born into a musical family. He was influenced by Johnny Mooring, and has made 2 LP's. Bridgewater, N.S.

George Hruska has played fiddle and drums in several orchestras, including 22 shows at Expo '86. He has won several contests. Gerald, Saskatchewan.

Bill Irving is a prominent fiddler and contest player in southern Ontario. His wife is an excellent pianist. He has made one LP. Mitchell, Ontario.

Don Isenor is from N.S.

Kimberly Isenor is from Milford Station, N.S.

Claude Jacob, still a teenager, is one of many superb fiddlers to come out of the cultural "melting pot" of Valleyfield, Quebec, just south-west of Montreal. Competitions and jamborees in this area bring together the best of rural and urban Quebec and the best of western Quebec and eastern Ontario. Grande Ile, Quebec.

Chuck Joyce began fiddling at nine, inspired by his father. He is one of Canada's outstanding contest fiddlers, winning in Shelburne in junior and later champion class. In four different contests including Pembroke, he came first three years in a row and has won numerous other contests across North America. He plays guitar, banjo, mandolin, piano, and bass, appears on TV, radio and shows, is a judge and teacher. London, Ontario.

Ernie Joyce is Chuck Joyce's father. Deceased.

Robert Joudrey inherited a fiddle from his grandmother and learned fiddle listening to Don Messer on radio. He has played for dances, won many contests and composed numerous tunes. He has combined a love of fiddling and heritage by, for example, producing a book "Bluenose Facts and Fiddle Tunes" in which the descriptions of the tunes explain the history of south-east Nova Scotia. Lunenburg, N.S.

Kevin Kienlein made a cassette in which he played fiddle, guitar, banjo, dubro and did the recording and arrangements. He is one of several professional composers who is making 'traditional' fiddle music modern by writing rags and stomps in traditional style, music for the fox trot or jive. Vernon, B.C.

Patti Kusturok began playing classical violin at four, began fiddle at six and began entering contests the same year. She won the Manitoba Junior Championship six years in a row and has won open contests in Ontario, Manitoba and Alberta. Winnipeg, Manitoba.

Eugene Laderoute began learning fiddle at seven from his father. He wrote 33 tunes, made two records and won numerous contests, including the Manitoba open. He died of a heart attack just after winning first prize in Killarney, Manitoba, and 40 fiddlers played at his funeral. He was born in Ste. Rose, Manitoba.

Bobby Lalonde came from a musical family, began fiddling at eight and performed with his three brothers. He was taught by the late Johnny Mooring, and influenced by Ward Allen and Graham Townsend. When Prime Minister Trudeau hosted world leaders at an Economic Summit in Montebello, Quebec, he invited Lalonde to play for them. He has gone on to become one of Canada's top songwriters and band leaders, winning prizes such as instrumentalist of the year, and has made numerous LP's. Fournier, Ontario.

Denis Lanctôt began playing fiddle at age 7, and plays piano, accordion, guitar, mandolin and banjo. He began entering contests at 14 and has won over 100 prizes, including first at Pembroke, 2nd at Shelburne, and the Maritime Open three times. He represented Canada at the 1982 Knoxville World Fair and the 1986 Vancouver World Fair. Ottawa.

Ned Landry is one of the half dozen "greats" of Canadian fiddling. An Acadian from New Brunswick, he is a master of every style, including Calypso and cajun. He is one of few who can fiddle and stepdance at the same time. He began playing with Don Messer at age 11, later formed the New Brunswick Lumberjacks band, toured North America for years with Don Messer, Hank Snow, Johnny Cash and Wilf Carter. He won twice at Shelburne, and has made over 30 LP's. St. John, N.B.

Harold Langille helped found fiddling organizations in Bridgetown and Lunenburg, has organized festivals, workshops and fund-raisers and supported the publications of books of fiddle music. Lunenburg, N.S.

Frank Leahy, Waterloo, Ontario, is a member of the famous musical Leahy Family of Peterborough (uncle Frank and cousin Donnell are also fiddlers and composers). Waterloo, Ontario.

Garry Lepine lives in Portage la Prairie, Manitoba.

Cy Lovell played fiddle and mandolin in the 1930's, including his own compositions on CBC. He had a radio program for one year, and played with Andy Dejarlis. He is now a successful competition contestant, a judge, and violin-maker. Summerland, B.C.

Dan MacCormack learned to play fiddle by ear at five from his father, and at 56 learned to read music. He is a member of the PEI Fiddlers Society, whose 150 fiddlers revived and promoted fiddling on the island. They play in the Cape Breton style, have two LP's and perform in concerts, cultural events and senior citizens' homes. St. Eleanors, P.E.I.

Bill MacInnis (Sr.) began playing fiddle at six–his father was a fiddler. He is left-handed, and has an orchestra. Village Green, P.E.I., C0A 1Z0.

Billy MacInnis (Jr.) began playing at five, played for his first dance at seven. Accompanied by John Allan Cameron, he played to a crowd of 6000 in Charlottetown, and he has played on CBC. He dedicated a composition to Duke Nielsen who played bass for Don Messer for 40 years. Village Green, P.E.I.

Hector MacKenzie, played guitar and fiddle at numerous dances in one-room schools, eventually playing on radio and TV. He is deeply involved in the Iona Highland Village, an organization dedicated to preserving Celtic culture. He has helped produce books of fiddle music and his music has been recorded by his brother Carl and the Highland Village. Iona, N.S.

John Afton McLellan is a fourth-generation fiddler. He played in lumber camps in the 1920's, has played all over Nova Scotia and was a frequent entertainer in senior citizens' homes. Halifax, N.S.

Natalie MacMaster began playing fiddle at 9 and played for a concert at 10. She has played in various parts of Canada and the U.S.A., and plays piano as well as doing stepdancing and Highland dancing. Port Hastings, N.S.

Roma McMillan learned classical violin and played in the Monteral Symphony. As a farmer's wife in southeast Ontario, she began playing fiddle music at dances. She has produced records and a book, won a hundred trophies, taught fiddling for years (to Ed Whitcomb), and organized groups of her own students to play at senior citizens' homes and concerts. She is a main organizer of the Ottawa Winter Fair Contest, of other events, and still plays with the Nepean Symphony Orchestra. Ottawa.

Margaret MacPhee learned music and stepdancing a half century ago from her parents, uncles, grandparents and neighbors. At that time hardly anyone owned a piano and she taught herself to play. Her son, Doug, is a master of the unique Cape Breton style of playing both the chords and the melody. He is in charge of the music collection at Cape Breton College. New Waterford, N.S.

Jack McTavish played fiddle in Manitoba. Deceased.

Clayton Magee began playing fiddle at 15, and has won numerous contests. He has been on radio, TV and played for 5 years with the Bluegrass band "The Down East Partners". He has made one cassette. Petitcodiac, N.B.

Keith Malcolm was born in Ottawa and moved to British Columbia via the U.S.A. He began classical violin, then mastered a number of fiddle styles. He is a highly successful performer with old-time, Scottish country, and ethnic bands and at folk festivals and is a champion-class contestant. Victoria, B.C.

Bill Meeks, began playing fiddle in the late 1930's but was interrupted by World War II. He resumed playing the 1950's, his band "Billie Meeks and the Party Gang" performed at dances and parties. Gravenhurst, Ontario.

Marcel Meilleur began playing at 14 and was back-up fiddler for Andy Dejarlis for 14 years. From 1976-80 he did a CBC program "Les Echoes de la Riviére Rouge". He has made over 40 LP's and his music reflects his Métis background. Winnipeg, Manitoba

Don Messer began playing fiddle at six and played for his first dance at seven. His influence on Canadian fiddling has been profound. (Please see section on Prince Edward Island in the essay on fiddle music.) Deceased.

Charles Milne lives in Manitoba.

Mark Moore learned to play fiddle in 1938 and joined a group called Smokey Joe and his Tune Wranglers in 1946. He later played with The Rancheros and the Rhythm Ramblers, and on radio. He has won several contest trophies. Sarnia, Ontario.

Matilda Murdoch taught herself how to play fiddle at age eight, learned how to read music at 16, and began composing tunes in the 1950's (over 100) that are played from North America to Ireland. Her two LP's are used extensively by stepdancers, and she has won numerous contests and has judged from Ontario to the Maritimes. Loggieville, N.B.

Hugo Oberg began learning violin in Sweden and immigrated to Manitoba with his family in 1912. He studied music writing in University and plays with the Hanley Old Time Fiddlers. Maple Ridge, B.C.

Don Pettigrew took up fiddling at 29. As a member of the Ontario Provincial Police, he has protected and entertained people all over Ontario. Thunder Bay, Ontario.

Carl Plohman taught himself to play at age 12 and was playing in an orchestra for dances and weddings within two years. He has won over 100 trophies, including the Manitoba Championship three times. He plays with the "Country-Tyme Band" and his compositions have been recorded by his daughter, Crystal. Glenboro, Manitoba.

Crystal Plohman began playing fiddle at six, entered her first competition one year later, and has won over 200 trophies. She has made 3 LP's.

Lionel Poirier was a fiddler from the Moncton area of New Brunswick who wrote the Island Ferry, named for the ferry that unites North America to P.E.I.

Bob Ranger is the most famous stepdance fiddler in the Ottawa Valley. He is one of many Canadian fiddlers who would quit work for half an hour to listen to the Don Messer show on radio. He is one of few fiddlers who could later pick up his fiddle and play the tunes he had heard. Ottawa.

Angus Robichaud has played fiddle all his life in New Brunswick. He was recorded as early as 1944 and again by Ivan Hicks Moncton, N.B.

Frank Rogers is one of Canada's best country and western fiddlers. He did ten seasons with CTV's Chuckwagon Show, toured the U.S.A., for five summers with Rex Allen, and has played with Lorne Green, George Jones, Webb Pierce, Ray Price and Jim Reeves. He toured Canada, Australia and Switzerland, and made 10 LP's. Mission, B.C.

Keith Ross is a professional musician who has played harmony in country groups for over 30 years. He has won contests from British Columbia to Nova Scotia and has toured in the U.S.A. He owns a music store in New Minas, N.S.

Dan Rubin was trained on classical violin and plays fiddle, mandolin, mountain dulcimer, bouzouki, guitar, cello-guitar, pianolin, autoharp and piano. He plays with a trio "New Earth" which specializes in jazz folk fusion. Victoria, B.C.

Robert Scheller is from Manitoba.

Oliver Schroer, a professional musician, has made videos to promote old-time fiddling, won numerous contests, plays and writes traditional fiddle and is composing "modern" fiddle music that is expanding the horizons of traditional music. He has made one cassette. Toronto.

Louis Schryer is one of the three famous triplets from Sault Ste. Marie. He, brothers Dan and Pierre, and older brother and fiddle maker Raymond dominate the championship class throughout central Canada, and sister Julie is one of the best pianists. Their list of trophies and accomplishments (one LP) and appearances is endless, and through teaching they are beginning to produce a second generation of Schryer-style fiddlers (Dan is Kai Whitcomb's teacher.) Ottawa.

Llewellyn McPherson (Max) Sexsmith began playing fiddle at six, learning it and guitar from his father and uncle. He began playing for dances during the depression for one dollar or less a night in British Columbia. He played with the Blue Ridge Boys, the Rhythm Ranch Hands and the Caribou Old Timers for two decades, including a regular show on radio. He is one of the founders of the British Columbia Old Time Fiddle Association and has made one LP. Prince George, B.C.

Winston Simpson is a great promoter of fiddling in Manitoba, the organizer of the Miami festival. He appeared for years on a radio show. Miami, Manitoba.

Earl Smith learned fiddle in 1919 from a violinist in the Winnipeg Symphony. He played in many orchestras, and played with friends at both ends of the run on the Ontario Northland Railway (he was an engineer). He is typical of the selfless dedication of fiddlers and of the absence of any "generation gap" among musicians. He once heard a brilliant young fiddler play and encouraged her to continue–Patti Kusturok's music is also in this book. Brandon, Manitoba.

Gerry Smith is one of the pre-eminent fiddlers of southwest Ontario. He is a stepdance fiddler and has won novelty and regular contests all the way to the west coast, is a judge, and has passed his love of music to his children (Linda is the pianist on his records). He has published several books of music. Exeter, Ontario.

Ervan Sonier has played fiddle for 55 years. He is one of the founding members of the PEI Fiddlers Association and has toured with them from B.C. to France and Spain. Summerside, P.E.I.

Cye Steele has played fiddle in New Brunswick and across Canada for two generations, appearing with numerous bands (the Stealaways) and on numerous recordings including his own LP's and on radio and TV. He entered the Maritime Open 20 consecutive years, and won it in 1959. He is working on a book of fiddle music. Brookfield, N.S.

Brenda Stubbert comes from a family of fiddlers in Cape Breton, won a trophy for piano playing at nine and began fiddling one year later. The "school of music" she attended is typical of many Cape Breton fiddlers: the best fiddlers were frequent guests in her father's (Robert's) house, which explains why the Cape Breton tradition is so solid, comprehensive and self-perpetuating. Port Aconi, N.S.

Lloyde Tattrie at age 77 plays in a bluegrass band, the "Harmony Trial", and they are planning a cassette. He played for dances for over 50 years, won numerous trophies, and played on National CBC. Tatamagouche, N.S.

Adélard Thomassin is one of many Quebecers who has devoted his life to the preservation and promotion of French Canadian musical culture. He has been involved in every possible aspect of culture since the 1940's: dance and music, composing, playing, producing, radio and TV, recordings, contests, carnivals, festivals, cultural exchanges between provinces and in France, Spain, Belgium, Holland and Yugoslavia. He reflects the fact that in Quebec (as in modern Scotland) fiddle music and accordion music are often the same. Sillery, Quebec.

Todd Thompson began playing at age eight (1978), and studied both old-time and classical violin. He entered his first competition the year he began playing fiddle, and at age 18 had competed in Shelburne for 10 consecutive years. He has won approximately 30 trophies and written over 15 tunes. Petrolia, Ontario.

Eleanor Townsend is the only woman to have ever won the North American Fiddle Championship in Shelburne in its 40 years. She has carried that undefeated title since 1979. Star of CBC Radio, TV, stage and recordings, she works with Graham and also as a solo act. She has performed with many of the same people that Graham has performed with. Eleanor is an inductee in the North American Fiddlers Hall of Fame, Osceola, New York, has recorded four solo albums and numerous albums with Graham, and has composed about 50 fiddle tunes. She has become the best known teacher of fiddle music and will be publishing the first of a series of books on her method of teaching this year. People have studied with her from as far away as British Columbia, Alberta, and New York State. Her playing has been called graceful, stately and elegant - and yet still old-time. Eleanor would like to take this opportunity to thank her fans and friends for their support through the years, with a special thank-you to Graham, her family and her manager, Brian Edwards of Rocklands Talent. Willowdale, Ontario.

Graham Townsend, a living legend in the music world. There has been no other fiddle player who has made the achievements that Graham has made. He is a five-time undefeated North American Fiddle Champion; star of CBC, TV, radio, stage, recordings, and films. He has just recently appeared in the highly acclaimed motion picture Beautiful Dreamers. Graham has done two Royal Command Performances for H.M. Queen Elizabeth, July 1st, 1967, Parliament Hill, Ottawa, Canada and September, 1982, Commonwealth Games, Brisbane, Australia…travelled and toured in 12 different countries…performed with such people as Hank Snow, Wilf Carter, Carol Baker, Tommy Hunter, Hagood Hardy, K.D. Lang, Sylvia Tyson, Stompin' Tom Connors, Allan Thicke, Gordie Tapp, Dinah Christie, Don Messer, Rhythm Pals, Maurice Bolyer, Porter Wagoner, Jimmy Dickens, Billy Walker, Kitty Wells, Roy Acuff, Dolly Parton, Mac Wiseman, Grandpa and Ramona Jones, George Jones, Buck Owens, Johnny Cash, Bill Munroe, Forrester Sisters, and list could go on. He has recorded 36 albums to date, is an inductee into the North American Fiddlers Hall of Fame, Osceola, New York, guests every year at the Grand Masters Fiddle Competition, Nashville, Tennessee. He is the composer of over 350 fiddle tunes, and this year will be inducted into the Country Music Hall of Fame, Ottawa, Canada, and also celebrates 35 years in the music business. Graham would like to take this opportunity to thank his fans for their support through the years, and a special thanks to his manager, Brian Edwards of Rocklands Talent. These are just some of the reasons that he is called 'The man with the magic bow' and 'The master of it all'.

Kelli Trottier comes from a musical family in Glengarry Country, Ontario, and began playing fiddle and classical violin at nine. She has competed and won from Ontario to the Maritimes and the U.S.A., and plays and stepdances at the same time. She is studying music at University and teaches fiddling. Kingston, Ontario.

Norman Truman began playing fiddle in the 1930's and began entering contests forty years later. Saskatoon, Saskatchewan.

Norman Tully, Hants County, N.S.

Jessie Wardle is from Manitoba.

Don Whynot is one of the founders of the Lunenburg County Fiddlers, south of Halifax, Nova Scotia. He has played with Hank Snow who is from the same area, and has won 15 contests. Bridgewater, N.S.

Harold Wright is a left-handed fiddler who has played in competitions for 25 years, winning the Manitoba Open. Portage la Prairie, Manitoba.

Cape Breton Jigs

Alex Graham's Jig

by Margaret MacPhee

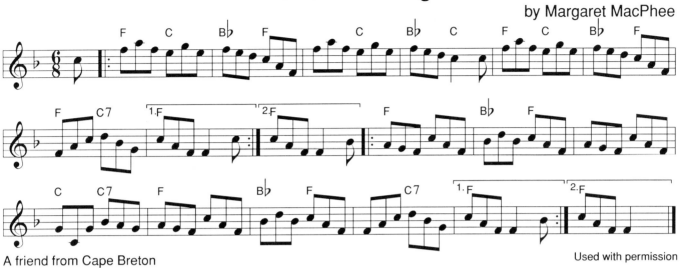

A friend from Cape Breton

Jeanette (MacDonald) Beaton's Jig

by Margaret MacPhee

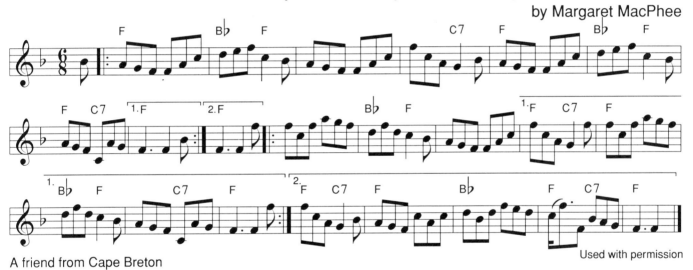

A friend from Cape Breton

Margaret MacPhee's Jig

by Margaret MacPhee

Jacqueline's Jig

by Margaret MacPhee

Margaret MacPhee's daughter, Jacqueline

Doug's Jig

by Margaret MacPhee

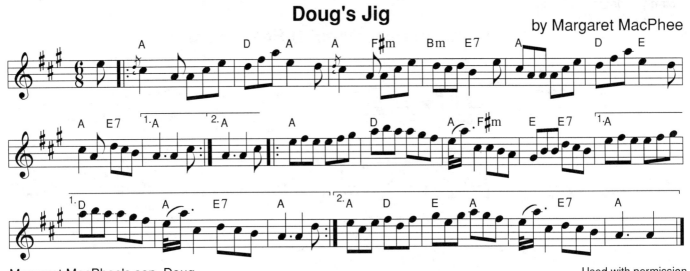

Margaret MacPhee's son, Doug

Josie MacArthur's Jig

by Margaret MacPhee

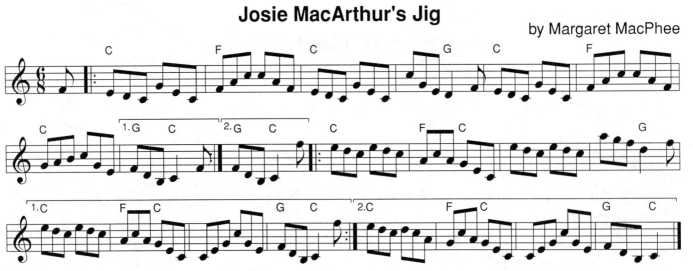

A friend from Taylor, Michigan

26

Wilbert Stubbert's Jig

by Brenda Stubbert

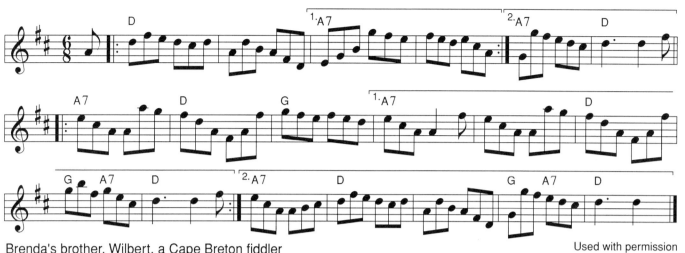

Brenda's brother, Wilbert, a Cape Breton fiddler

Launchie Stubbert's Jig

by Brenda Stubbert

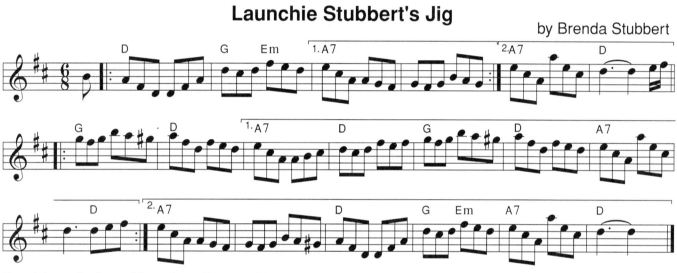

Brenda's uncle, Launchie, a Cape Breton fiddler

Regina Stubbert's Jig

by Brenda Stubbert

Brenda's mother, Regina

Memories of Donald Angus Beaton Jig

by Elizabeth Beaton

Elizabeth's husband, Donald Angus

Used with permission

One for the Record

by Natalie MacMaster

Composed for Natalie's first record

Used with permission

Compliments to my Dad

by Brenda Stubbert

Robert Stubbert, Cape Breton fiddler

Used with permission

Lissie's Jig

by David B. Greenberg

Elizabeth Schulze, violinist

Used with permission

Francis Xavier Kennedy MacDonald (Jig)

by David B. Greenberg

Kenny MacDonald, Hamilton, Ontario

Used with permission

Charlene's Jig

by Hector MacKenzie

Hector's niece, Charlene

Jacinta's Jig

by Hector MacKenzie

Hector's niece, Jacinta

Mother's Day Jig

by Kinnon Beaton

Cape Breton Strathspeys

The Merry Miss Mary D. (Strathspey)

by David B. Greenberg

A friend at Indiana University, Mary Doeringer

In Step with Harvey (Strathspey)

by David B. Greenberg

Harvey Beaton, Cape Breton step dancer

Wendy's Lament (Slow Strathspey)

by David B. Greenberg

David's sister, Wendy

Dan R.'s Favourite Strathspey

by D. A. Beaton

Dan R. MacDonald, Cape Breton fiddler

Reprinted from Donald Angus Beaton's "Cape Breton Scottish Violin Music."
Used with permission

Willie Fraser's Strathspey

by D. A. Beaton

Willie Fraser, Cape Breton stepdancer

Reprinted from Donald Angus Beaton's "Cape Breton Scottish Violin Music."
Used with permission

MacPhee Hospitality (Strathspey)

by Kate Dunlay

Margaret and Doug MacPhee, Cape Breton pianists

Used with permission

Cape Breton Reels

Danny MacDonald of Hamilton's Reel

by Kinnon Beaton

Danny MacDonald, a guitarist from Hamilton

Used with permission

Maggie Ann's Reel

by Kinnon Beaton

For Maggie Ann Beaton, Mabou, N.S.

Used with permission

The Hughie & Allan Reel

by Kinnon Beaton

Hughie and Allan, Cape Breton Comedians

Used with permission

The Bare Feet Reel

by Natalie MacMaster

Used with permission

Mike and Marlene's Reel

by Natalie MacMaster

Used with permission

Fleagh Bat Beag

by David B. Greenberg

Pseudo-Gaelic for Bb minor, composed to compensate for the absence of reels in that key.

Honda Breakdown (Reel)

by David B. Greenberg

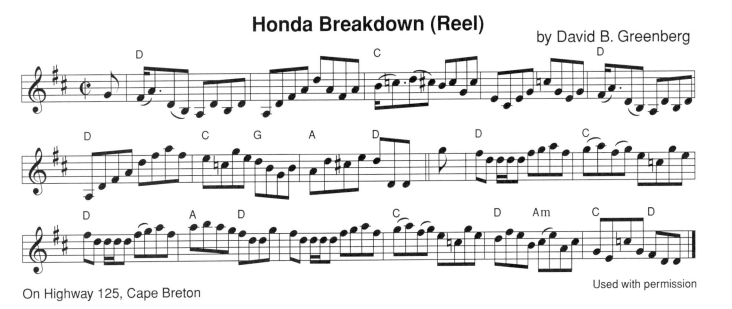

On Highway 125, Cape Breton

Jerry Holland (Reel)

by David B. Greenberg

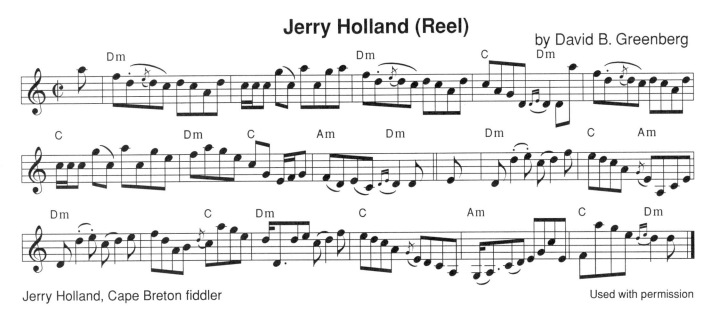

Jerry Holland, Cape Breton fiddler

A Reel for Kate

by David B. Greenberg

Kate Dunlay, David's wife   [♮♭ = between ♭ and ♯]

Finlay's Cheer

by David B. Greenberg
and Kate Dunlay

Finlay Walker, Cape Breton fiddler

A Toast to Danny Sandy (Reel)

by Kate Dunlay

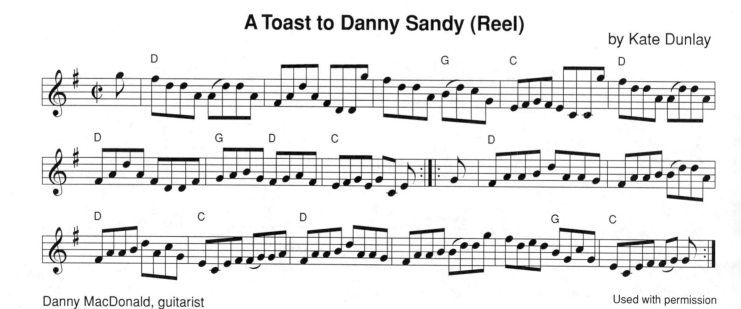

Danny MacDonald, guitarist

Expo Reel

by Natlie MacMaster

Composed for Expo '86, Vancouver

Cape Breton Marches and Clogs

Tracey Reginas: March

by Brenda Stubbert

Brenda's daughter, Tracey Regina, a stepdancer

Little Joey Gillis' March

by Kinnon Beaton

For Joey Gillis, Creignish, N.S.

Memories of Joe Confiant March

by Brenda Stubbert

Joe Confiant, a friend and Cape Breton fiddler

Doug MacPhee's Clog

by D.A. Beaton

Doug MacPhee, Cape Breton pianist

Two-Steps
Trail Blazers Two-Step
by Graham Townsend

Graham was on the road, trail blazing in western Canada

Used with permission

Bald Eagle Two-Step
by Robert E. Joudrey

Used with permission

One for Francis (Two-Step)
by Matilda Murdoch

Matilda's husband, Francis

Used with permission

Bow and Arrow Two-Step

by Robert E. Joudrey

Used with permission

The Mink Lake Two-Step

by Webb Acheson

Used with permission

Joyal's Two-Step

by Denis Brisson

Dedicated to Denis' son

Used with permission

Rick Hansen Two Step

by Kevin Kienlein

Rum Runners' Two-Step

by Robert E. Joudrey

Used with permission

Pat's Two-Step

by John Arcand

Used with permission

Roy and Nancy's Two-Step

by Bill Guest

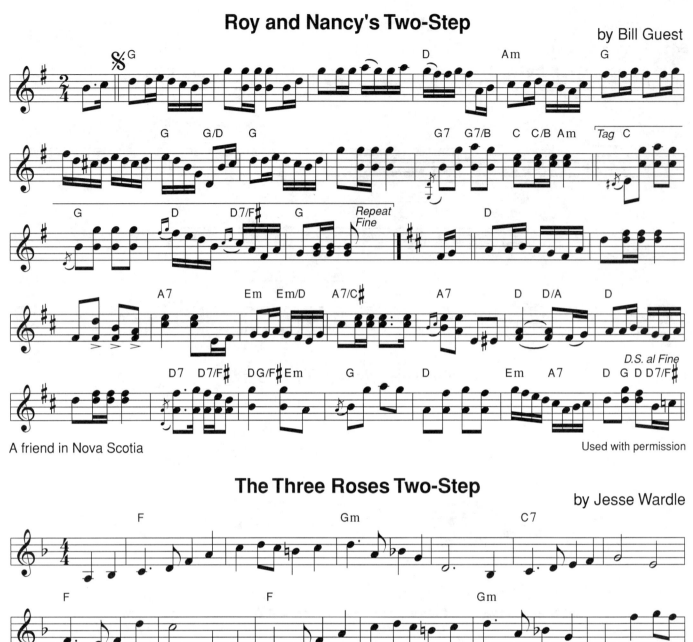

A friend in Nova Scotia

Used with permission

The Three Roses Two-Step

by Jesse Wardle

Used with permission

Polkas
Roy Acuff Special

by Ned Landry

A famous American musician

Used with permission

Al Cherney Special

by Ned Landry

Al Cherney, one of Canada's greatest fiddlers, died in 1989

Used with permission

Stompin' Tom Connors

by Ned Landry

The famous Stompin' Tom is Ned's cousin

Used with permission

43

Happy Time Fiddler

by Ken Davidson

Used with permission

The Haunted Fiddle

by Ken Davidson

Used with permission

The Three Sisters Polka

by Gordie Carnahan

Three mountains seen from Canmore, Alberta

Used with permission

Walter Ostanek's Polka

by Ned Landry

Used with permission

Pizza Polka

by Lawrence A. Buckler

Title inspired by a TV commercial

Used with permission

Olive's Polka

by Robert R. Scheller

Used with permission

The Tiger Hills Polka

by Carl Plohman

The Tiger Hills in southwestern Manitoba

Used with permission

Shirley's Polka

by Carl Plohman

Mrs. Carl (Shirley) Plohman

Used with permission

Holiday Polka

by Kevin Kienlein

Used with permission

Fred and Wilma's Polka

by John Arcand

Used with permission

Emma Lake Polka

by John Arcand
and Calvin Vollrath

Used with permission

San's Polka

by Jesse Wardle

Used with permission

Cacomistle Polka

by Paul Gitlitz

Paul's wife's pet, Cacomistle

Used with permission

Love on Samhain

by Paul Gitlitz

Samhain is the Celtic word for Hallowe'en

Used with permission

48

Clogs and Schottisches

George McKenny's Favorite

by Denis Lanctôt

A great supporter of fiddle music, Ottawa

Irish Fancy Clog

by Ron Gain

Jacquot's Clog

by Marcel Meilleur

Used with permission

Little Neil's Clog

by Crystal Plohman

Crystal's cousin, Neil.

Used with permission

50

Janet's Clog

by Matilda Murdoch

Janet Murdoch, Matilda's Granddaughter

Owen's Clog

by Matilda Murdoch

Owen Murdoch, Matilda's son

Smitty's Clog

by Earl Smith

Fine

D.S. al Fine

Used with permission

Vallyfield Clog

by Claude Jacob

Used with permission

A town south-west of Montreal

Ault Island Clog

by Roma McMillan

An Island in the Saint Lawrence River near Upper Canada Village

Used with permission

Golden Jubilee Schottische

by Abbie Andrews

Used with permission

Wardle's Schottische

by Jesse Wardle

Used with permission

Robert's Favorite Schottische

by Robert R. Scheller

Used with permission

53

Rags

Maytime Swing

by Graham Townsend

Composed in May

Bobcaygeon Swing

by Oliver Schroer

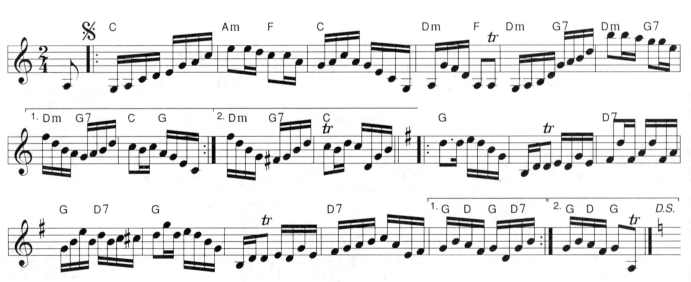

Bobcaygeon, Ontario, site of Ontario open fiddle competition

Happy Carolyn

by Gerald Hamilton

Carolyn Woods, pianist from Fergus, Ontario

Fergus Rag

by Gerald Hamilton

Fergus, north of Guelph, Ontario

Swingin' Jim Johnson's
Birthday Blues (Rag)

by David B. Greenberg
chords by Larry Hamberlin

Jim Johnson, guitarist

Used with permission

Dad's Day '87 (Rag)

by David B. Greenberg
chords by Larry Hamberlin

Leon Greenberg

Used with permission

Essie's Ragtime Swing

by Earl Smith

Essie Smith, pianist

Used with permission

Laying the Tile

by Earl Smith

Composed while watching a friend working

Used with permission

Cajun Rag

by Kevin Kienlein

Used with permission

Fiddle Boogie

by Kevin Kienlein

Used with permission

Fiddlers Rag

by Kevin Kienlein

Used with permission

Centerville Stomp

by Kevin Kienlein

Used with permission

Cheslatta Lake Rag

by Max Sexsmith

A lake in British Columbia

Pricin' the Blues

by Kevin Kienlein

Miscellaneous

Leningrad Lament

by Bill Guest

© Copyright by Bill Guest
Used with permission

Margaret Jean's Lament

by Bill Guest

A friend in Nova Scottia

Used with permission

61

Notes of Woe

by Lawrence A. Buckler

Slow and mournful

Composed while ill

Used with permission

Banks of Waugh

by Lawrence A. Buckler

The Waugh River, near Tatamagouche, N.S.

Used with permission

Variations on a Classical Theme

by Lawrence A. Buckler

Inspired by a classical theme

Used with permission

An Air for Kate

by David B. Greenberg

Kate Dunlay, David's wife

Togo Farewell (slow Waltz)

by David B. Greenberg

David's sister, Lise, leaving for Togo, West Africa

Patti Fiddles the Blues

by Ken Davidson

Used with permission

I Live Alone

by Marcel Meilleur

(The only fox trot in this book)

Used with permission

Abbie Andrews Calypso

by Ned Landry

Abbie Andrews is a fiddler from St. Catharines, Ontario

Used with permission

Happy Time

by Ned Landry

Used with permission

Cajun Fiddlin' on the Bayou

by Ned Landry

Used with permission

Sunset on the Ottawa

by Brian Hebert

Shades of Dawn

by Brian Hebert

Thomas Graham Stewart

by Paul Gitlitz

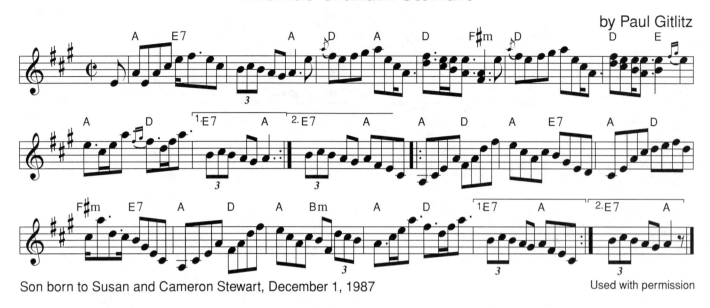

Son born to Susan and Cameron Stewart, December 1, 1987

Used with permission

Patty's Journey Home

by Paul Gitlitz

A lament for an ill friend

Used with permission

The House in the Meadow (Air)

by Dan Rubin

For Jane McKay's house warming

Farewell to Alan (The Camel) Karmazyn

by Paul Gitlitz

Lament for a fine actor and writer

Used with permission

Cyprus Winds

by Kevin Kienlein

Used with permission

Waltzes
Nancy's Waltz

by Bill Guest

A friend in Nova Scotia

Shelley's Waltz

by Bill Guest

Shelley Crawford, Halifax

Little Andrea's Tune

by Bill Guest

A friend in Nova Scottia

Pelican Waltz

by Bill Guest

Happy Birthday Waltz

by Dave Bagnell

Used with permission

71

Elmsdale Waltz

by John A. McLellan

Used with permission

Autumn Leaves Waltz

by John A. McLellan

Used with permission

Lorimer's Waltz

by Lorimer M. Higgins

Used with permission

Nancy Reetta Waltz

by Lorimer M. Higgins

Used with permission

Tidal Bore Waltz

by Lorimer M. Higgins

Famous tide in the Bay of Fundy

Used with permission

73

Cape John Waltz

by Lloyd Tattrie

Cape John, N.S.

Used with permission

MacDonald's Waltz

by Lloyd Tattrie

Mr. and Mrs. R. MacDonald, Joney River, N.S.

Used with permission

The Hula Hoop Waltz

by Robert E. Joudrey

Used with permission

Waltzing Around the Pumpkins

by Robert E. Joudrey

Used with permission

Waltz for Mary Ann

by Harold E. Langille

Mrs. Mary Ann (Harold) Langille

Elmwood Waltz

by Harold E. Langille

Harold Langille's hometown, N.S.

Ron Noiles Waltz

by Ken Davidson

A fiddler and music collector, Halifax

Waltz for Ward Allen

by Ken Davidson

Ward Allen, one of Canada's greatest fiddlers

Waterfall Waltz

by Roddy Dorman

Used with permission

B's Waltz

by Keith Ross

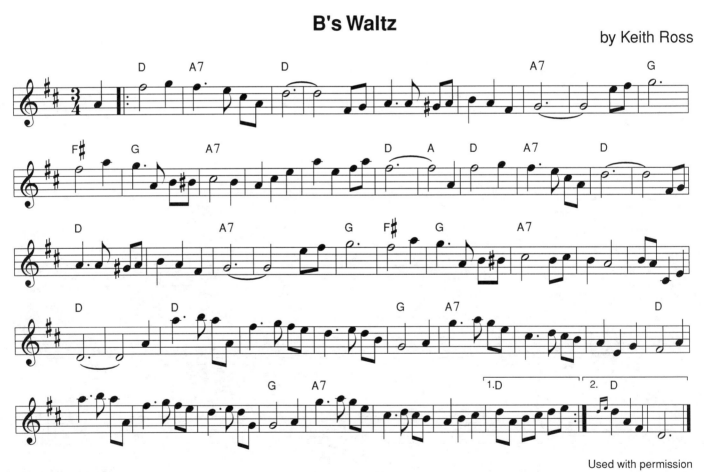

Used with permission

The Calgary Fiddlers Waltz

by Ned Landry

The Calgary Fiddlers have toured extensively in Canada

Used with permission

Waltzing in the Garden

by Ned Landry

Used with permission

Purple Violet Waltz

by Ivan Hicks

The provincial flower of New Brunswick

Evening Star Waltz

by Matilda Murdoch

Leonard's Waltz

by Beth Fenton

Northern Light Waltz

by Matilda Murdoch

Moonlight Waltz

by Matlida Murdoch

The Bill Guest Waltz

by Carl Elliott

Bill Guest, pianist, composer, teacher, publisher, Halifax. N.S.

Used with permission

Donna's Waltz

by Lawrence A. Buckler

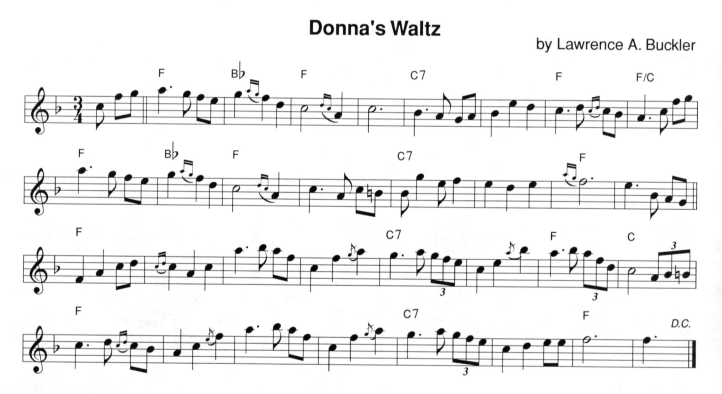

Composer's daughter, Donna

Used with permission

Chanya's Waltz

by Clayton Magee

Clayton's daughter, Chanya

The Royal Canadian Legion Waltz

by Cye Steele

Duke Nielson Memorial Waltz

by Billy MacInnis

Duke Nielson passed away in November, 1986

Ralph and Norma Porter's Waltz

by Bil MacInnis

Ralph and Norma Porter, Springhill, N.S.

Linda Marie Waltz

by Gerry Smith

Taky's Tune

by Ken Davidson

Used with permission

Doris' Waltz

by Yvon Cuillerier

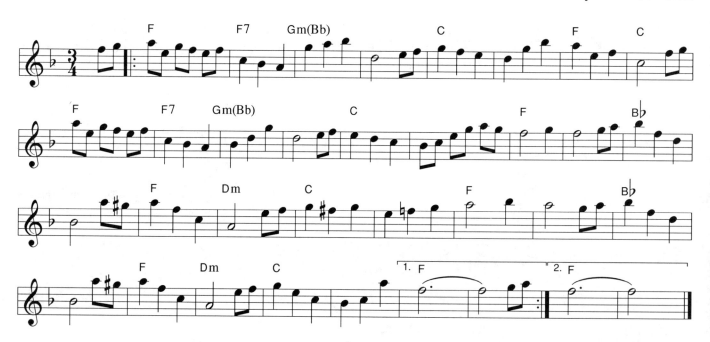

Used with permission

The Ashton Rose

by Leo Browne

Knitters' Waltz

by Bruce Armitage

Children's Waltz

by Brian Hebert

Used with permission

Raemona

by Brian Hebert

Brian's wife

Used with permission

1) Variation

Riverside Waltz

by Don Pettigrew

Riverside (Fiddle) Park, Pembroke, Ontario

Used with permission

92

The Nation River Waltz

by Denis Brisson

The Nation River joins the Ottawa River south-east of the nation's capital

Used with permission

Edna's Waltz

by Denis Brisson

Denis' wife

Used with permission

Carnival Waltz (Embrum Carnival Waltz)

by Denis Brisson

This waltz was composed for the Embrun Carnival

Used with permission

93

Sweet Sixteen Waltz

by Kelli Trottier

Kelli's sister, Tracy

Transcribed by Malcolm Dewar

Used with permission

94

Forget Me Not

by Don Pettigrew

Composed for Ruthanna MacPherson, pianist, Glengarry County, Ontario

Blue Sea Waltz

by Bobby LaLonde

95

Centennial Rose Waltz

by Gerald Bailey

Used with permission

Gene's Waltz

by Gerald Bailey

Used with permission

Loujo Waltz

by Webb Acheson

97

Debbie's Waltz

by Graham Townsend

Debbie MacDowell, a stepdancer

Used with permission

Waltz of the Bells

by Eleanor Townsend

Gordan and Mary Bell, supporters of old-time fiddling

Used with permission

98

Gerald's Waltz

by Gerald Bailey

Used with permission

Cheryl Susan's Waltz

by Graham Townsend

Daughter of Walter Ostanek, Canada's polka king

Used with permission

99

Big Ben Waltz Clog

by Gerry Smith

Used with permission

Anne Marie Waltz

by Mark W. Moore

Used with permission

Harvey Lovie's Waltz

by Chuck Joyce

Used with permission

Glengarry's Home to Me

by Carol (Kennedy) Dawson

Glengarry County, south-east of Ottawa

Used with permission

101

Sheguiandah Bay

by Don Pettigrew

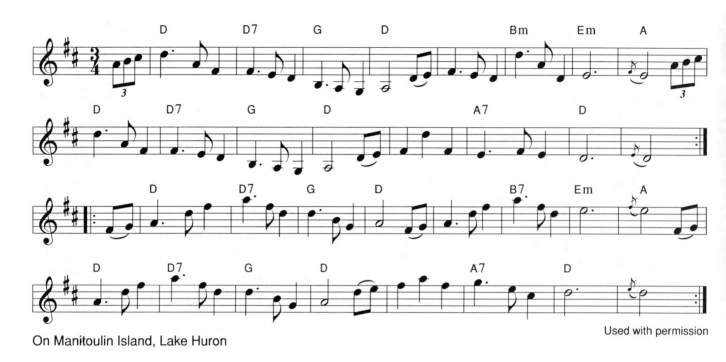

On Manitoulin Island, Lake Huron

Used with permission

Wilhelmine's Rose

by Don Pettigrew

Whilhelmine operated a tourist camp at Sheguiandah Bay

Used with permission

Leila's Waltz

by Don Pettigrew

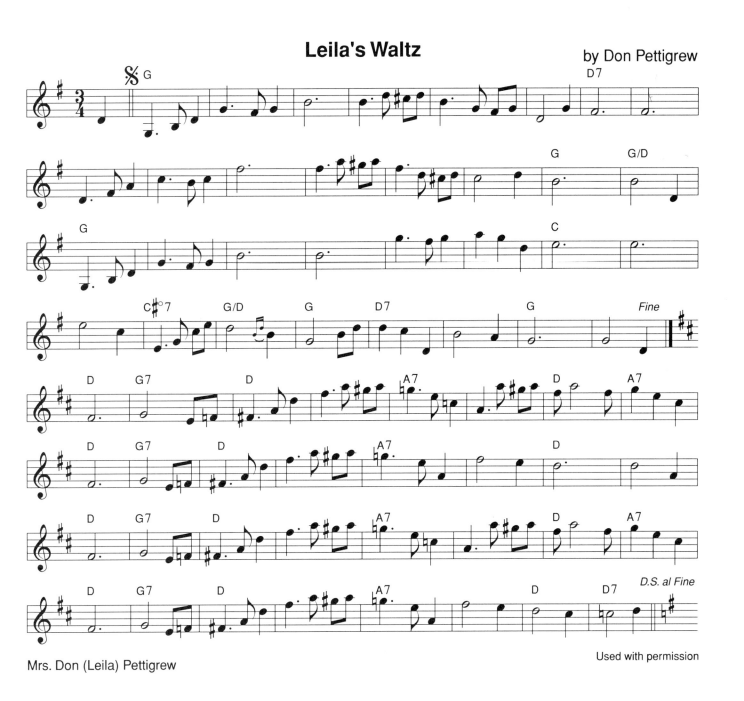

Mrs. Don (Leila) Pettigrew

Used with permission

Margaret Nixon's Waltz

by Don Pettigrew

Margaret Nixon, Vankleek Hill, Ontario

Used with permission

Millie's Waltz

by Oliver Schroer

Millie Parlee, a fan of old-time music

Our Last Waltz

by Ron Gain

Colonel By Waltz

by Roma McMillan

Colonel By built the Rideau Canal

Used with permission

Happy Go Lucky Boy Waltz

by Mel Bedard

Used with permission

The Selkirk Centennial Waltz

by Reg Bouvette

A town north of Winnipeg, centennial in 1982

Mose's Waltz

by Marcel Meilleur

Used with permission

Martin Lepine's Waltz

by Gene Laderoute

A member of Laderoute's band

Used with permission

John Stovin's Waltz

by Gene Laderoute

Used with permission

Albertine's Waltz

by Gene Laderoute

Used with permission

Marcel's Waltz

by Marcel Meilleur

Used with permission

108

The Blue Hills Waltz

by Gene Laderoute

Hills south of Brandon, Manitoba

Used with permission

Gene's Waltz

by Gene Laderoute

Used with permission

Eva's Waltz

by Patti Kusturok

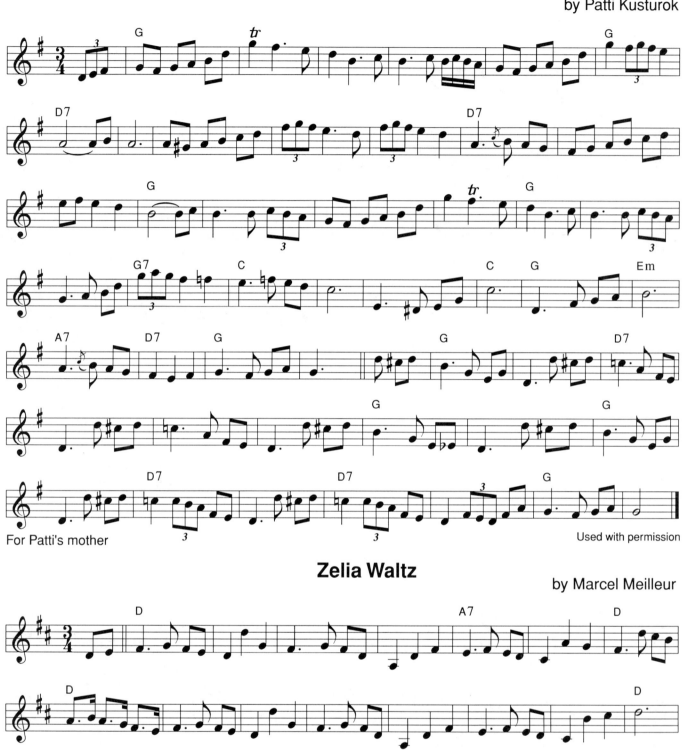

For Patti's mother

Used with permission

Zelia Waltz

by Marcel Meilleur

Used with permission

Carl's Waltz

by Carl Plohman

Used with permission

The Blue Taurus Waltz

by Harold Wright

Used with permission

The Williamson Lake Waltz

by Gordie Carnahan

Near Belmont, Manitoba

Used with permission

by Marcel Meilleur

Hometown Waltz

Used with permission

Marie's Waltz

by Jesse Wardle

Used with permission

The Waltz of the Prairies

by Jesse Wardle

Used with permission

The Melita Waltz

by Art Champion

Town in southwestern Manitoba

Used with permission

Heidi's Waltz

by Art Champion

Heidi Mickelson, North Dakota

Used with permission

The Meadowlark Waltz

by Gordie Carnahan

Used with permission

Jack's Waltz

by Jack McTavish

The McTavish Waltz

by Jack McTavish

The Thresherman's Waltz

by Duncan Emerson

Used with permission

Springtime in Manitoba

by Duncan Emerson

Used with permission

The Antler River Waltz

by Norman Cheyne

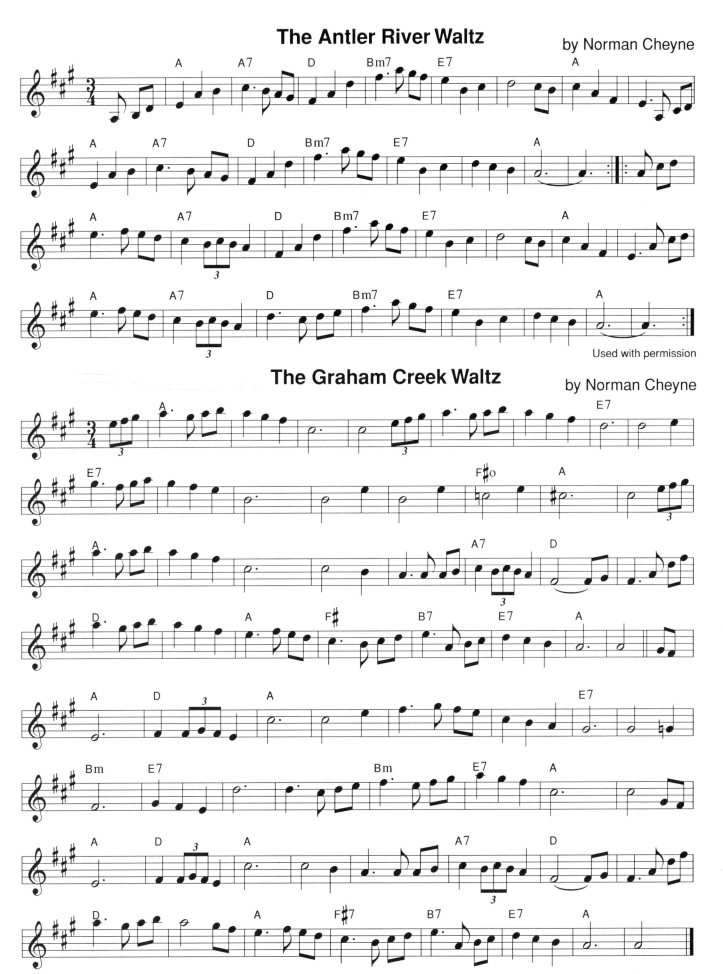

Used with permission

The Graham Creek Waltz

by Norman Cheyne

Used with permission

The Blue Lakes Waltz

by Cam Chernecki

Used with permission

The Greenwood Waltz

by Cam Chernecki

Used with permission

The Dusty Waltz

by Cam Chernecki

Used with permission

Charlie Milne's Waltz

by Charlie Milne

Used with permission

119

The Carman Waltz

by Winston Simpson

A town in southern Manitoba

Used with permission

The MacGregor Waltz

by Bob Emerson

A town in southern Manitoba

Used with permission

120

Brandon's Centennial Waltz

by Earl Smith

Brandon's Centennial, 1982

Used with permission

The Retired Railroader's Waltz

by Earl Smith

Earl was an engineer for 35 years

Used with permission

Alli's Waltz

by Dave Hepworth

The Lanark County Waltz

by Gordie Carnahan

Lanark County, west of Ottawa

Kathy's Waltz

by Dave Hepworth

Used with permission

The Mayfield Waltz

by Dave Hepworth

Used with permission

Captain Cole's Waltz

by Dan Rubin

Captain Cole, Gulf Islands ferry (Vancouver-Lasqueti Island)

Melancholy Meadows

by George Hruska

Named for disappearing meadowlands

K-Country

by George Hruska

K is for potash, a major
Saskatchewan resource

Used with permission

* alternate

Waltzing with Someone

by Kevin Kienlein

Used with permission

The Campbellini's Waltz

by Keith Malcolm

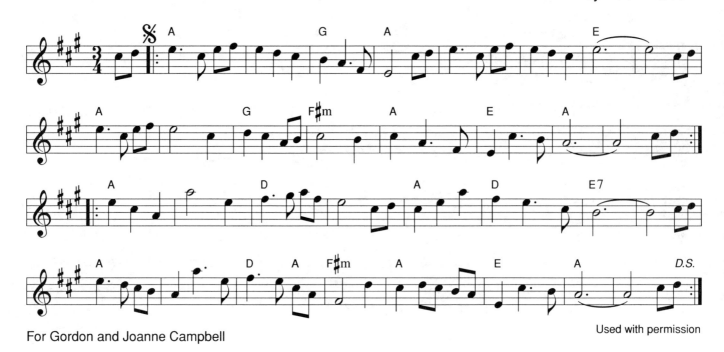

For Gordon and Joanne Campbell

Used with permission

Carolyn's Waltz

by Keith Malcolm

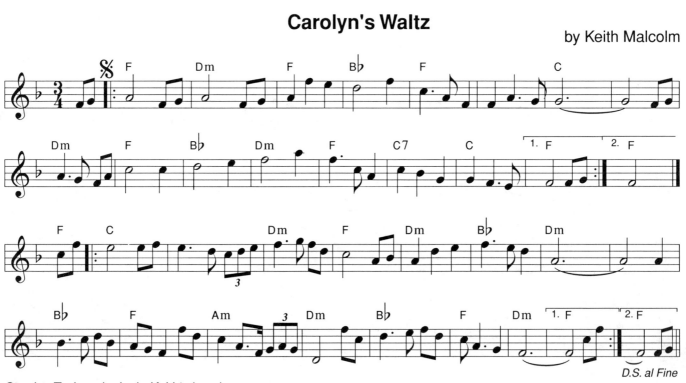

Carolyn Taylor, pianist in Keith's band

Used with permission

Kate's Waltz

by Keith Malcolm

A friend of the composer

Gold Fiddle Waltz

by Frank Rodgers

First prize in some contests is a gold fiddle

Used with permission

The Haney Old Time Fiddlers Waltz

by Hugo W. Oberg

Used with permission

Jigs
The Little Red Schoolhouse Jig
by Robert E. Joudrey

Used with permission

The Rainbow Jig
by Robert E. Joudrey

Used with permission

J.B. Jig
by Lawrence A. Buckler

Composer's wife, J. (Jean) B. (Buckler)

Used with permission

129

Lake Peter Jig

by Harold E. Langille

Used with permission

Texas Lake Jig

by Harold E. Langille

D.S. al Fine
Used with permission

LaHave River Jig

by Donald Whynot

River in N.S.

Used with permission

130

Skip's Jig

by Kimberly J. Isenor

Used with permission

Brogan's Cove Jig

by Mac Brogan

Used with permission

131

Baie Ste Anne Quadrille

by Angus Robichaud

A bay in New Brunswick

D.S. al Fine

Used with permission

Kent County Jig

by Angus Robichaud

Used with permission

Tracey's Jig

by Lorimer M. Higgins

Used with permission

East Point Jig

by Matilda Murdoch

Near Loggieville on the Miramichi River, N.B.

D.S. al Fine

Used with permission

Marg's Jig

by Matilda Murdoch

Marg Scott, pianist from Ottawa

Used with permission

Gemma's Jig

by Dan MacCormack

Mrs. Gemma (Dan) MacCormack

Used with permission

The Duke Nielson Jig

by Bill MacInnis, Jr.

Duke Nielson played bass fiiddle for Don Messer for 40 years

Montreal Jig

by Yvon Cuillerier

Expo '86 Jig

by Yvon Cuillerier

Quadrille Thomas

by Adélard Thomassin

Used with permission

Jungle Jane's Jig

by Kelli Trottier

Kelli's high school principal, Jane Wright   Transcribed by Malcolm Dewar

Used with permission

Peter's Jig

by Kelli Trottier

Kelli's husband, Peter   Transcribed by Malcolm Dewar

Used with permission

Royal Wedding Jig

by Brian Hebert

The wedding of Prince Charles and Diana

Shady Nook Jig

by Brian Hebert

A village south of Pembroke, Ontario

Onslow Jig

by Bruce Armitage

Misty

by Webb Acheson

Used with permission

Blackie's Jig

by Denis Brisson

A friend's dog

Used with permission

The Welder's Jig

by Bob Ranger

Amongst other things, Bob is a welder

Transcribed by Malcolm Dewar

Used with permission

137

Canada Council Jig

by Roma McMillan

The Council supports all forms of culture in Cananda (including this book)

Ottawa Girls' Jig

by Roma McMillan

Upper Canada Jig

by Roma McMillan

The old name for Ontario

Murray River Jig

by Graham Townsend

Murrary River, P.E.I.

Used with permission

Gray's Second Change

by Graham Townsend

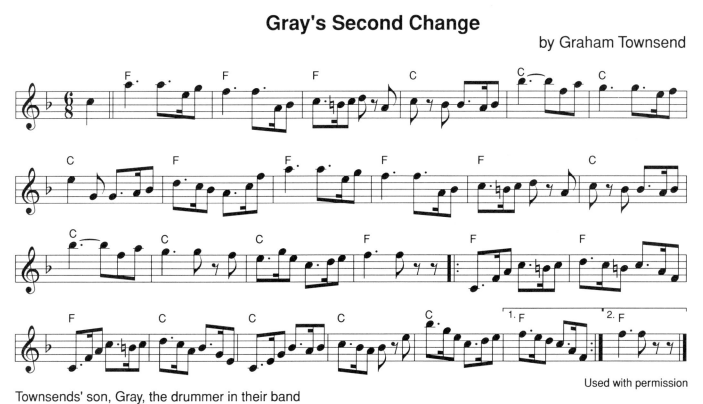

Used with permission

Townsends' son, Gray, the drummer in their band

139

Dungannon Sweetheart

by Graham Townsend

Eleanor is from Dungannon, Huron County, Ontario

Frank Kelly's Jig

by Eleanor Townsend

A square-dance caller from Toronto

Sam's Suger Bush Jig

by Gerry Smith

Composed while camping on Lake Huron

Lemonville

by Jack Hayes

Used with permission

Carm Oliver's Jig

by Jack Hayes

Used with permission

Kathy's Fraser's Jig

by Jack Hayes

Used with permission

Richmorra

by Jack Hayes

Used with permission

Kari's Jig

by Oliver Schroer

Kari Hudson, a friend

Used with permission

Bobby Brown's Jig

by Jack Hayes

Bobby Brown leads the Cape Breton Symphony

Used with permission

Mrs. Norah Coakley

by Jack Hayes

Used with permission

Fleming's Jig

by Ron Gain

Used with permission

G Minor Jig

by Gerald Bailey

Used with permission

Mountain View Jig

by Gerald Bailey

Used with permission

The Val - J - S Jig

by Gerald Bailey

Used with permission

144

Rocks on the Lawn

by Ian Hamilton

Used with permission

Squaw Lake Jig

by Ian Hamilton

Used with permission

Ernie's Special Jig

by Ernie Joyce

Used with permission

Echoes of Pembroke

by Bill Meeks

Pembroke, north-west of Ottawa, hosts one of Canada's best annual fiddle competitions

Used with permission

The Light Amber Jig

by Bill Meeks

Anyone who drinks rum will understand

Used with permission

Salmon Creek Jig

by Todd Thompson

Used with permission

Terry's Jig

by Mark W. Moore

Dedicated to my son Terry Douglas Moore

Used with permission

The Pleasant Valley Jig

by Ivan Fisher

Used with permission

The Fifty-Five Mile Jig

by Dan Rubin

Mile 55 on the British Columbia Railway, near Quesnel

Used with permission

The Spruce Woods Jig

by Carl Plohman

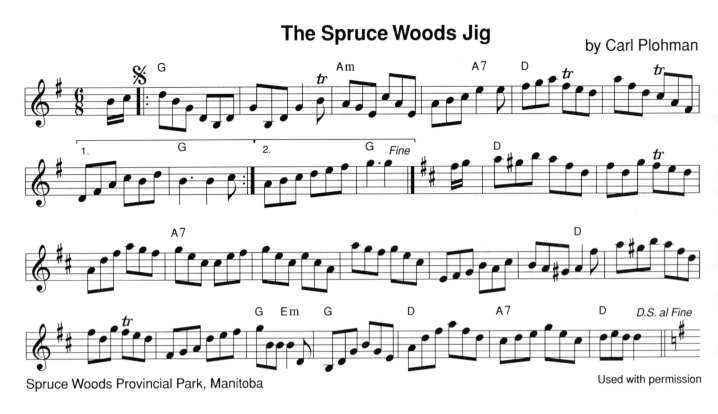

Spruce Woods Provincial Park, Manitoba

Used with permission

Grandpa's Jig

by Crystal Plohman

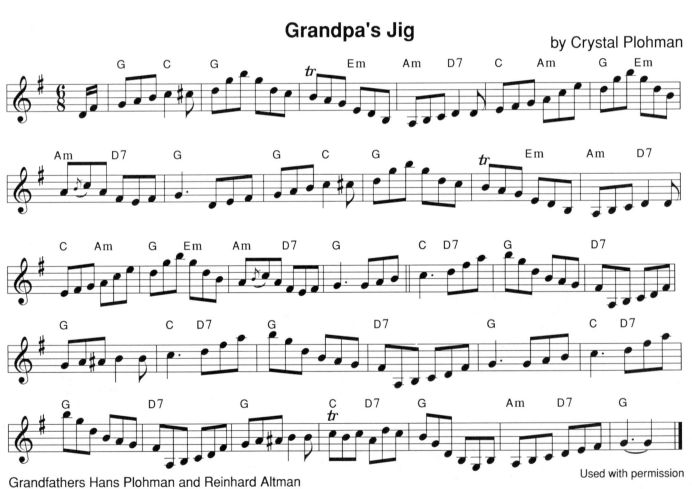

Grandfathers Hans Plohman and Reinhard Altman

Used with permission

The Beaver Creek Jig

by Harold Wright

Used with permission

The Springbrook Jig

by Norman Cheyne

Used with permission

The Sourisford Jig

by Art Champion

On the Souris River, southwestern Manitoba

Used with permission

149

Nor's Jig

by Jesse Wardle

Used with permission

Jesse's Jig

by Jesse Wardle

Used with permission

Joey's Jig

by Jesse Wardle

Used with permission

150

Armand's Jig

by Marcel Meilleur

Fine

D.S. al Fine

Used with permission

Traveller's Jig

by John Arcand

Used with permission

Medric McDougall's Instrument Change Jig

by John Arcand

Used with permission

151

The Rusty Nail

by Norman Truman

M & N Jig

by Norman Truman

Maggie and Norm, Mrs. and Mr. Truman

The Cowtown Jig

by Gordie Carnahan

Calgary is Cowtown, Canada

Used with permission

The Twenty Dollar View

by Gordie Carnahan

The mountains on the twenty-dollar bill

Used with permission

Myllie's Own Jig

by Myllie Barron

Used with permission

The Dagenais Special

by Gordie Carnahan

Robbie Dagenais, a fiddler from Pembroke, Ontario

Campsite Jig

by Max Sexsmith

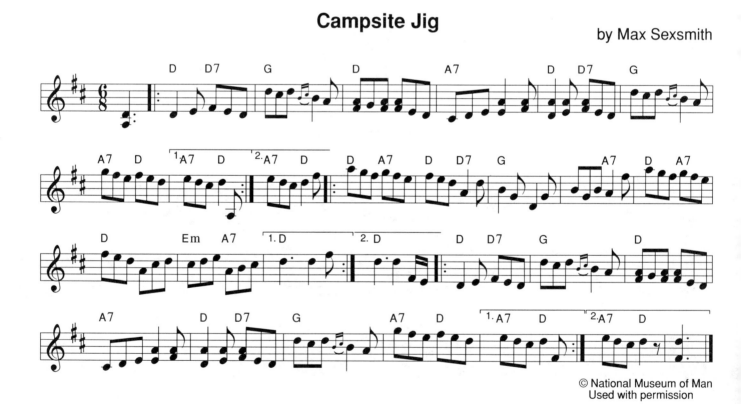

The Aloutte River Jig

by Hugo W. Oberg

Used with permission

Eggs on the Couch

by Paul Gitlitz

Hand-painted eggs

Used with permission

The Alma Centennial Jig

by Gordie Carnahan

Alma, south of Belmont, Manitoba

Used with permission

155

Bain's Jig

by Kevin Kienlein

Used with permission

Dancing on the Moors (Jig)

by Kevin Kienlein

Used with permission

Dominion Day Jig

by Kevin Kienlein

Used with permission

156

Carolyn's Jig

by Keith Malcolm

Carolyn Taylor, pianist in Keith's band

The One that Got Away

by Keith Malcolm

Joys of fishing

Bill Dundon's Jig

by Keith Malcolm

An Irish fiddler from Vancouver

Christine (McCann) Gautier Jig

by Wilf Gillis

Daughter of Des McCann, owner of Gentle Annie's Irish Pub, Ottawa

Used with permission

Gentle Annie's Irish Stew

by Wilf Gillis

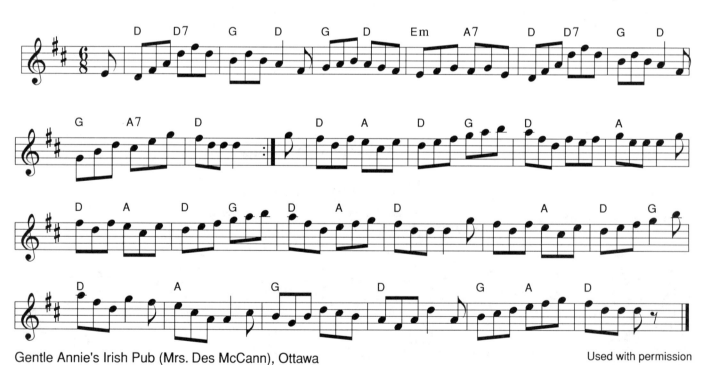

Gentle Annie's Irish Pub (Mrs. Des McCann), Ottawa

Used with permission

Breakdowns
Mel Fulford's Breakdown

by Cye Steele

Used with permission

Mac Brogan's Breakdown

by Mac Brogan

Used with permission

Wilfred Bishop's Breakdown

by Mac Brogan

Used with permission

The Crazy Fiddler's Breakdown

by Robert E. Joudrey

Mush-a-Mush Lake Breakdown

by Donald Whynot

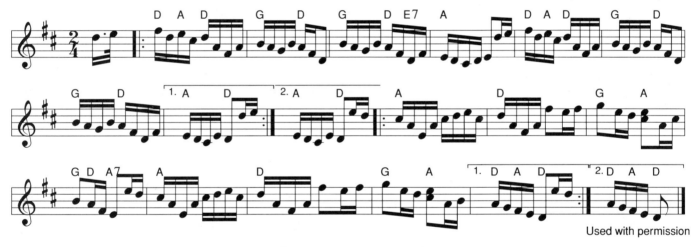

Rail Roaders' Breakdown

by Donald Whynot

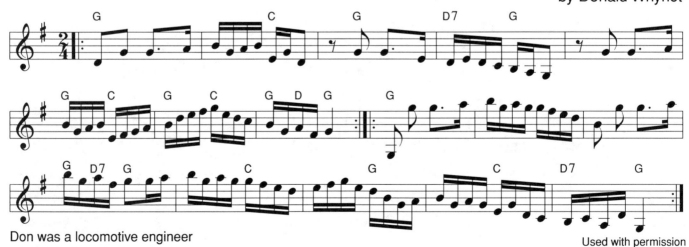

Don was a locomotive engineer

Norm Burgess Breakdown

by Ned Landry

Norm Burgess is director of the Calgary fiddlers

Used with permission

Semiwagon Breakdown

by Matilda Murdoch

On the Miramichi River, N.S.

Used with permission

Todd's Island Breakdown

by Jimmie Chapman

Home of Rodeo Records near Halifax, N.S.

Used with permission

161

Durelle's Victory Breakdown

by Angus Robichaud

Used with permission

Howie Getson's Breakdown

by Clayton Magee

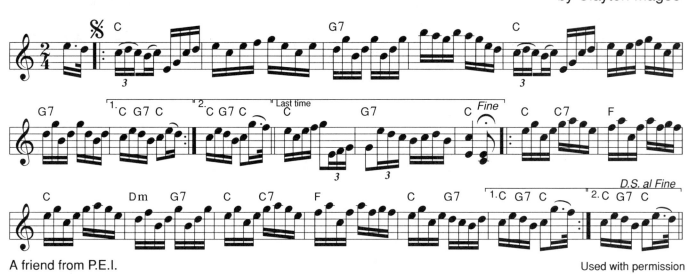

A friend from P.E.I.

Used with permission

The Parkland Breakdown

by Gene Laderoute

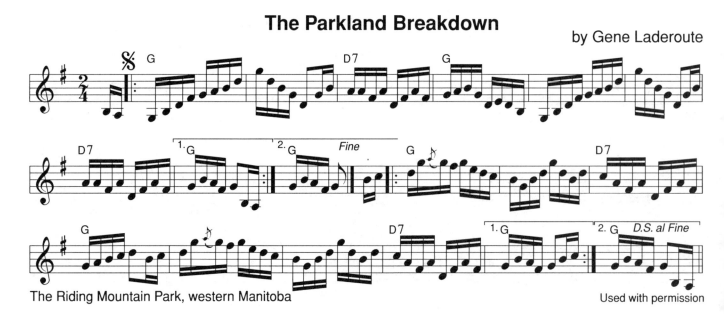

The Riding Mountain Park, western Manitoba

Used with permission

Schryer's Breakdown

by Louis Schryer

Used with permission

The Longford Breakdown

by Bill Meeks

Longford Township, near Muskoka, north of Toronto

Used with permission

Man O'War Breakdown

by Todd Thompson

Used with permission

163

Yvette's Favorite Breakdown

by Denis Encontre

Yvette Carriere, a Manitoban pianist

Used with permission

Emery's Breakdown

by Denis Encontre

Co-written with Denis' uncle, Emery

Used with permission

Last Minute Breakdown

by Denis Encontre

Composed just before recording a second album

Used with permission

Garry's Breakdown

by Garry Lepine

Used with permission

Wendy's Breakdown

by Gary Lepine

Used with permission

The Belmont Centennial Breakdown

by Gordie Carnahan

Belmont, Manitoba, Centennial 1989

Used with permission

165

The Barclay House Breakdown

by Windston Simpson

Used with permission

The Miami Breakdown

by Winston Simpson

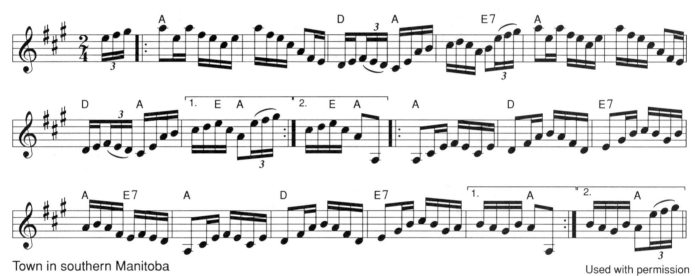

Town in southern Manitoba

Used with permission

The Crystal City Breakdown

by Bill Delorme

A town in southern Manitoba

Used with permission

Lac La Biche Breakdown

by John Arcand

Used with permission

Fiddlin' Farmer's Hoedown

by George Hruska

Intro and tag

Used with permission

Prince George Breakdown

by Max Sexsmith

Prince George, British Columbia

Valley Breakdown

by Cy Lovell

Reprinted from 141 Brand New Old Time Fiddle Tunes, Vol. 2

Hornpipes
John A. McLellan's Hornpipe

by Lloyd Tattrie

A fiddler from Elmsdale, N.S.

Used with permission

Jim Delaney's Hornpipe

by Lloyd Tattrie

Jim Delaney organizes the Maritime Old Time Fiddle Contest

Used with permission

The Halifax County Hornpipe

by Norman Tulley

Used with permission

Highland View Hornpipe

by Keith Ross

Used with permission

North King Street Hornpipe

by Donald Whynot

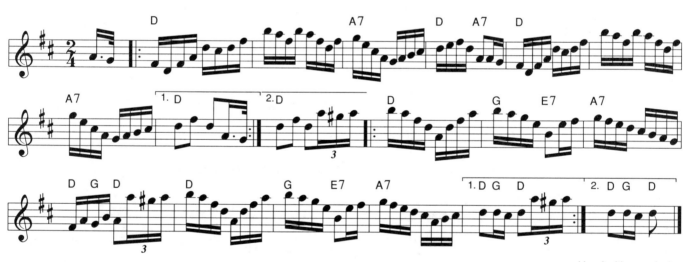

North King Street, Bridgewater, N.S.

Used with permission

Admiral's Hornpipe

by Bill Andrews

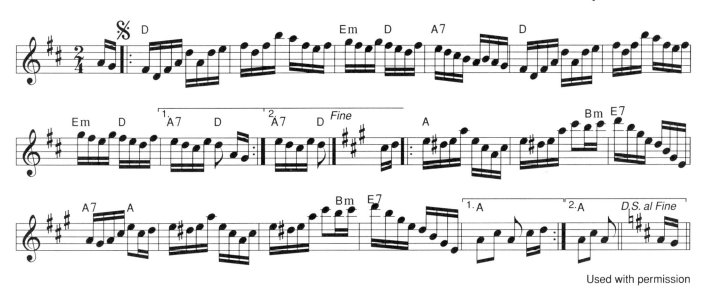

Fine

D.S. al Fine

Used with permission

The St. Rose Hornpipe

by Gene Laderoute

Used with permission

A town in central Manitoba

Ranger's Hornpipe

by Bob Ranger

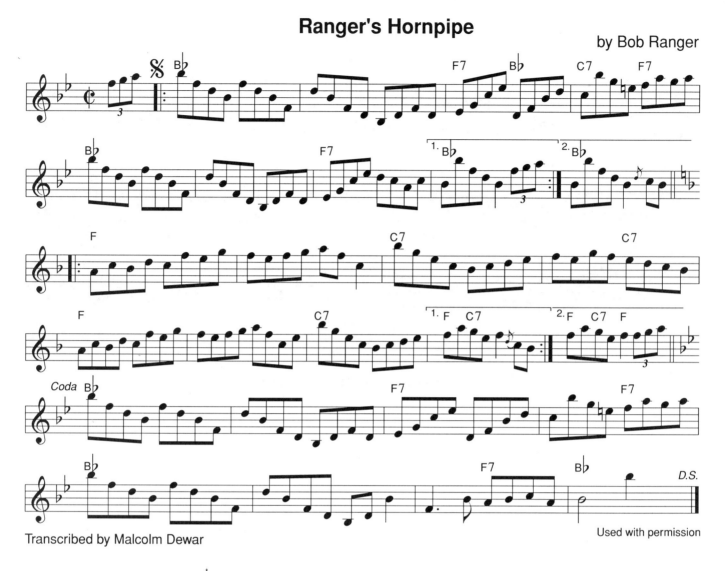

Transcribed by Malcolm Dewar

Used with permission

Lambton County Hornpipe

by Chuck Joyce

Used with permission

172

Sandy Cameron's Hornpipe

by John Arcand

Soaring Eagle Hornpipe

by John Arcand

The Toaster in the Closet

by Oliver Schroer

173

Cortez Island Hornpipe

by Keith Malcolm

An island near Victoria, B.C.

Used with permission

Bonaparte Crossing His Eyes

by Paul Gitlitz

Used with permission

Ed Whitcomb's Hornpipe

by Wilf Gillis

Ed Whitcomb, a fiddler from Ottawa

Used with permission

174

Reels

Centennial Highway Reel

by Rufus Guinchard

Canada's Centennial, 1967

Used with permission

Traveller's Reel

by Rufus Guinchard

Composed in 1930

Used with permission

Brendan's Bow (Reel)

by David B. Greenberg

Brendan Mulvihill, Irish fiddler, Baltimore, Maryland

Used with permission

175

Whirlygig Reel

by Bill Guest

Used with permission
© Copyright by Bill Guest

Thirteenth of January

by Bill Guest

Ending

Composed while playing Don Messer's fiddle

Used with permission
© Copyright by Bill Guest

Port of Halifax

by Roddy Dorman

Used with permission

Carl's Homecoming

by Lawrence A. Buckler

Carl Gamble, Debert, N.S.

Used with permission

Florence's Fiddle

by Lawrence A. Buckler

Florence Killen, Truro, N.S. One of the great supporters of fiddle music

Used with permission

Francis' Favorite

by Lawrence A. Buckler

Francis MacDonald, West Lawrencetown, N.S.

Used with permission

177

Mother Vera's Reel

by Lawrence A. Buckler

Composer's mother, Vera

Used with permission

Tip o' the Hat

by Lawrence A. Buckler

A gentlemanly practice of greeting people

Used with permission

Glenda's Reel

by Carl Elliott

Carl's daughter, Glenda

Used with permission

Hand Gliders' Reel

by Lorimer M. Higgins

Used with permission

Nova Scotia Reel

by Lorimer M. Higgins

Used with permission

Indian Lake Reel

by Harold E. Langille

Used with permission

179

The Island Ferry

by Lionel Poirier

Used with permission

The Draggers Reel

by Eddy Arsenault

Used with permission

The Seaweed Reel (Wandering Traveller)

by Ervan Sonier

D.S. al Fine

Used with permission

180

Tracey's Reel

by Clayton Magee

D.S. al Fine
Used with permission

Complainer's Reel

by Clayton Magee

Used with permission

Don Isenor's Party

by Dave Bagnell

Don Isenor, fiddler and composer, N.S.

Used with permission

Carbonelle Reel

by Matilda Murdoch

Ed Carbonelle, bass player, Almonte, Ontario

Used with permission

Kimberly's Reel

by Matilda Murdoch

Kimberly Murdoch, Matilda's granddaughter

Used with permission

Norman Tulley's Reel

by Don Isenor

Used with permission

Mactaquac Reel

by Don Messer

The Mactaquac Dam near Fredericton, N.B.

Used with permission

Stoney Reel

by Don Messer

The Stoney Indians, Alberta

Used with permission

Grace MacPherson's Reel

by Jimmie Chapman

Wife of the owner of Rodeo Records

Used with permission

Valleyfield Reel

by Yvon Cuillerier

A town south-west of Montreal

Used with permission

Sam Cormier Reel

by Denis Lanctôt

A fiddler from Chetticamp, Cape Breton

Used with permission

Fiddlers' Valley Reel

by Brian Hebert

Used with permission

Rolling Thunder Reel

by Brian Hebert

1) Variation:

Used with permission

Reel St. Jean-Baptiste

by Claude Jacob

Used with permission

Reel des Bardeaux de Cèdres

by Adélard Thomassin

Used with permission

185

Foresters Falls Reel

by Bob Ranger

A village near Lanark, Ontario

Transcribed by Malcolm Dewar

Used with permission

Wendy's Reel

by Kelli Trottier

Kelli's cousin, Wendy

Transcribed by Malcolm Dewar

Used with permission

Bernie's Reel

by Bob Ranger

Bernie is a close friend

Transcribed by Malcolm Dewar

The Embrum Reel

by Denis Brisson

A town south-east of Ottawa

Harvey's Tune

by Graham Townsend

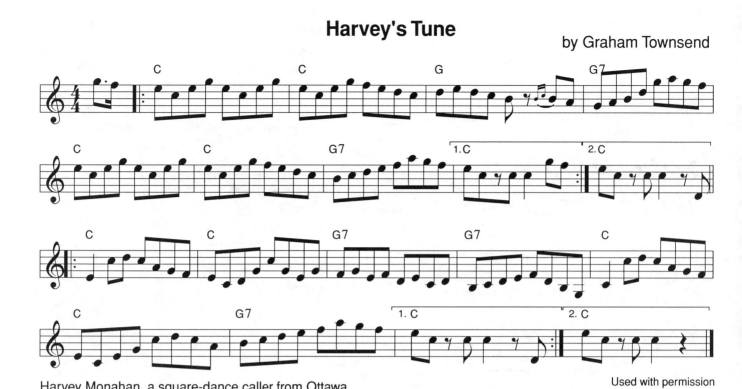

Harvey Monahan, a square-dance caller from Ottawa

Used with permission

Kimberly Mountain

by Bill Irving

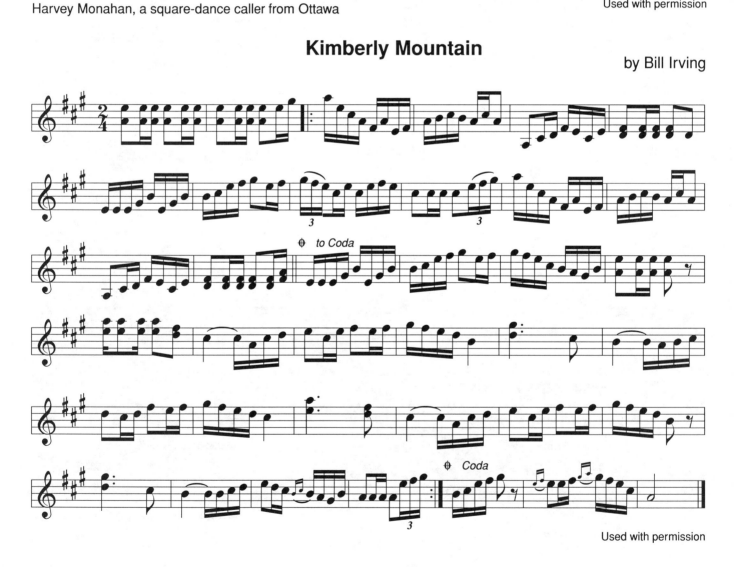

Used with permission

Cornyn Street

by Eleanor Townsend

Home of Earl Hayward, Wingham, Ontario

Used with permission

Native Reel

by Bill Irving

Used with permission

Anne's Reel

by Oliver Schroer

Anne Lederman, fiddler and professional musician, Toronto

Used with permission

The Road to Paris

by Oliver Schroer

For friends moving to Paris

Used with permission

Janet Munson's

by Oliver Schroer

A fiddler from Halifax

Used with permission

Allen's Reel

by Webb Acheson

Used with permission

Cactus Reel

by Webb Acheson

Used with permission

Webb's Favorite (Reel)

by Webb Acheson

Used with permission

191

Christopher's Reel

by Louis Schryer

Used with permission

Billie on the Tight Rope

by Bill Meeks

The sensation of working out the notes for a new reel

Used with permission

The Muskoka Homestead Reel

by Bill Meeks

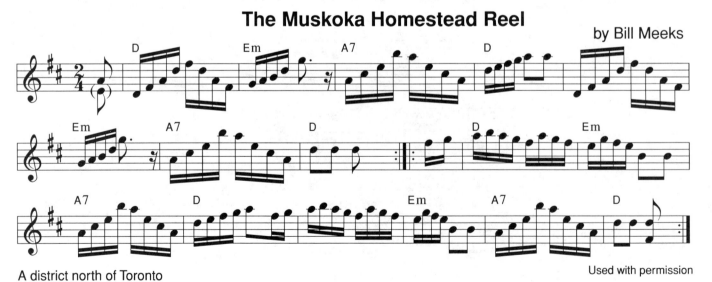

A district north of Toronto

Used with permission

The Golden Fawn

by Gerald Bailey

Used with permission

Silver Lake Reel

by Gerald Bailey

Used with permission

Lloyd McVeigh's Reel

by Ron Gain

Used with permission

193

Belle River Reel

by Frank Leahy

Near Sarnia, Ontario

Kirky's Reel

by Frank Leahy

In a Stew

by Frank Leahy

Karly's Edge

by Frank Leahy

Used with permission

Teeswater

by Frank Leahy

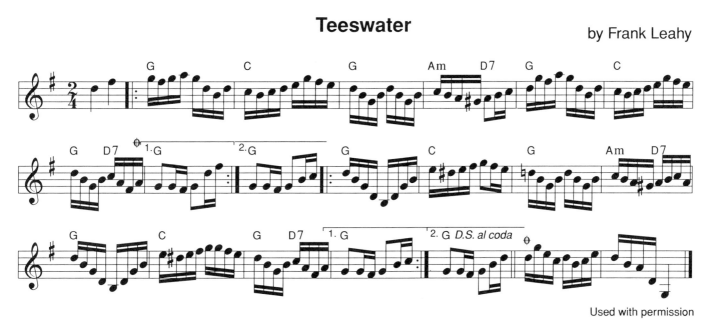

Used with permission

Walkers Special Reel

by Chuck Joyce

Used with permission

Chuck's Reel

by Todd Thompson

Used with permission

Mark of Mitten North

by Todd Thompson

Used with permission

196

Lord Alexander's Reel

by Abbie Andrews

Used with permission

The Wobbly Goose

by Abbie Andrews

Used with permission

Canadian Constitution Reel

by Roma McMillan

Used with permission

197

Ritchie Street

by Oliver Schroer

Home of Brian Pickell and Kate Murphey, Toronto

Misty's Reel

by Crystal Plohman

Crystal's dog, Misty

Patti's Reel

by Patti Kusturok

The Wanderer's Reel

by Harold Wright

Used with permission

Horner's Trophy Reel

by Harold Wright

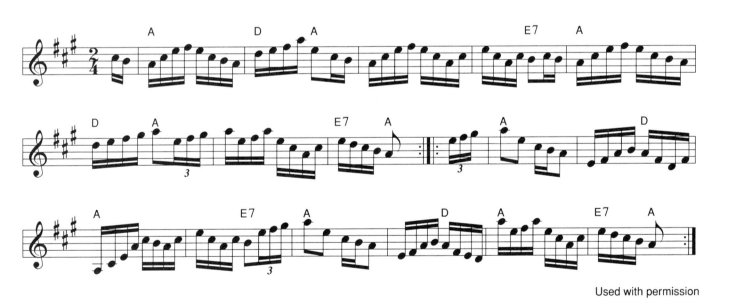

Used with permission

199

The Five Arch Bridge

by Gordie Carnahan

A stone bridge in Pakenham, near Ottawa

Used with permission

Armin's Reel

by Earl Smith

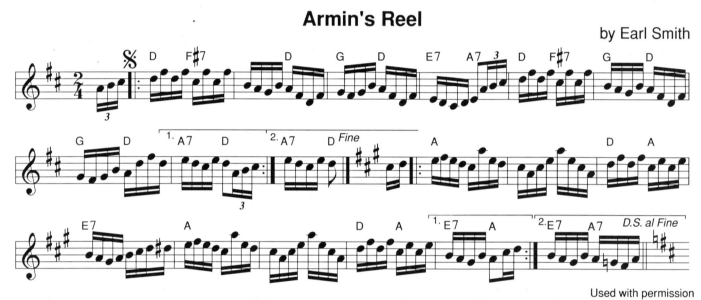

Used with permission

The Polar Bear Express

by Earl Smith

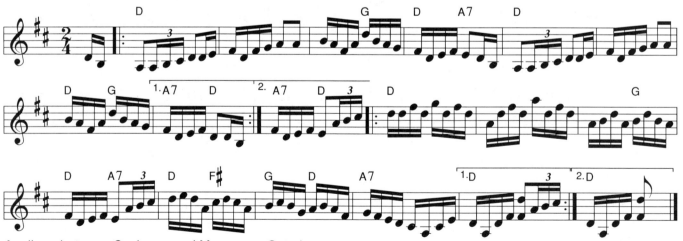

A railway between Cochrane and Moosonee, Ontario

Used with permission

200

The Boyne River Reel

by Winston Simpson

Used with permission

Lil's Favorite Reel

by Garry Lepine

Used with permission

Art Champion's Reel

by Art Champion

Used with permission

201

Festival du Voyageur Reel

by Marcel Meilleur

Used with permission

Guy's Special

by Marcel Meilleur

Used with permission

Meilleur Reel

by Marcel Meilleur

Used with permission

Red River Brigade

by Marcel Meilleur

Used with permission

Reel des Bois Brûlés

by Marcel Meilleur

Used with permission

War Bonnet Reel

by Marcel Meilleur

Used with permission

Foxey Donna

by Reg. Bouvette

Used with permission

Man with Two Tarps

by Mel Bedard

Used with permission

The Solar Eclipse

by Gene Laderoute

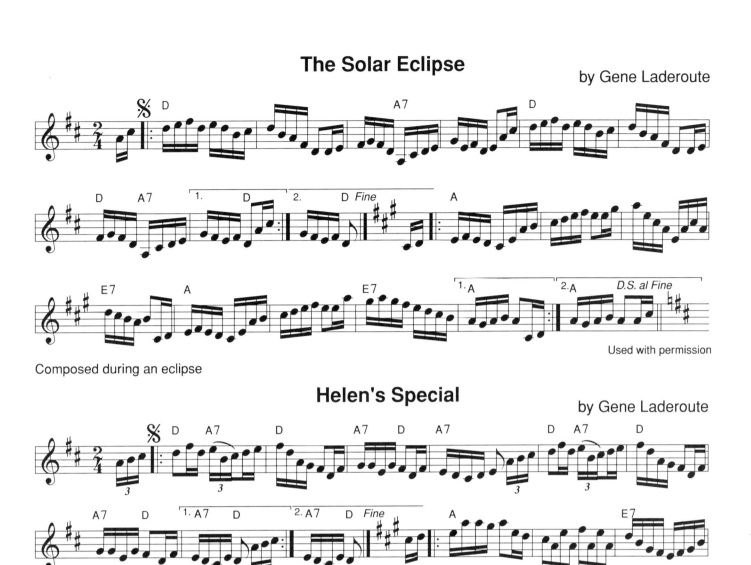

Composed during an eclipse

Used with permission

Helen's Special

by Gene Laderoute

Mrs. Helen (Martin) Lepine, a member of Laderoute's band

Used with permission

Grey Owl Reel

by John Arcand

Used with permission

205

Patti's Reel

by Dave Hepworth

Used with permission

Sir Galahad's Scart (Kitty in a Snit)

by Paul Gitlitz

For Paul's pet cat

D.C. al Fine

Used with permission

Cy's Favorite

by Cy Lovell

Reprinted from 141 Brand New Old Time Fiddle Tunes, Vol. 2

New Fiddle Reel

by Cy Lovell

Reprinted from 141 Brand New Old Time Fiddle Tunes, Vol. 2

Haymakers

by Cy Lovell

Reprinted from 141 Brand New Old Time Fiddle Tunes, Vol. 2

Blanche's Reel

by Myllie Barron

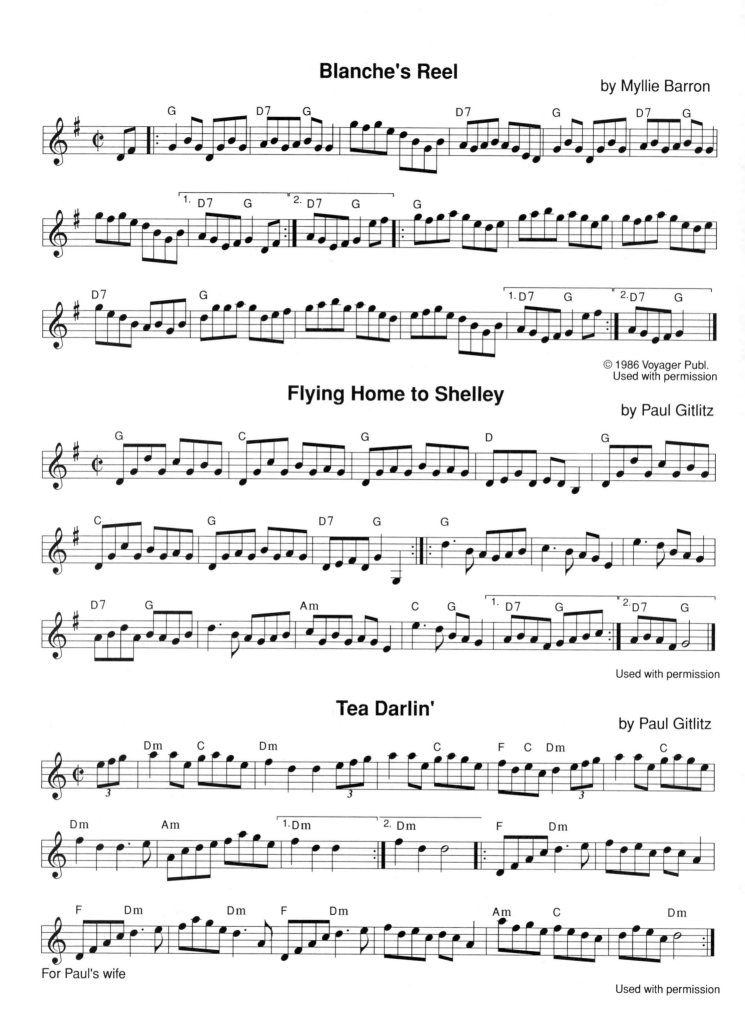

© 1986 Voyager Publ.
Used with permission

Flying Home to Shelley

by Paul Gitlitz

Used with permission

Tea Darlin'

by Paul Gitlitz

For Paul's wife

Used with permission

Composer Index

Index to Tunes

Hornpipes

Reels

Bibliography

There is extensive literature on Canadian fiddling and its origins. It includes books, theses, biographies, articles, information on records, newsletters of the fiddle associations and countless newspaper articles. Unfortunately there are huge gaps in this information, which makes writing a book like this very difficult. This bibliography is divided somewhat arbitrarily in three, Part I contains the material that was most useful for writing the book; Part II contains other information on fiddling; Part III lists books of fiddle music though there is a lot of music in some of the books identified in Parts I and II. (Some of the information on the items (dates, etc.) was not available).

Part I : Main Sources For This Study

Begin, Carmelle, *Jean Carignan*, Ph.D. thesis. Laval.

———*La Musique Traditionelle Pour Violin : Jean Carignan*, Museum of Man, Mercury Series, no. 40, Ottawa, 1981.

Emmerson, George, *Rantin Pipe and Tremblin String*, McGill-Queen's Press, Montreal, 1971.

Guest, Bill, *Canadian Fiddlers*, Lancelot Press, N.S., 1984

Dunlay, Kate, "The Playing of Traditional Scottish Dance Music : Old and New World Styles & Practices", Congress of Celtic Studies, St. Mary's University, Halifax, 1989.

Feldman, Allen & O'Doherty, Eamonn, *The Northern Fiddler*, Blackstaff Press, Belfast, 1979.

Hornby, Jim, *The Fiddle on the Island* (PEI), M.A. thesis, Memorial University, St. John's, 1983.

Johnson, David, *Scottish Fiddle Music in the Eighteenth Century*, John Donald, Edinburgh, 1984.

Lederman, Anne, *Native and Métis Fiddling in Two Manitoba Communities, Camperville and Ebb and Flow*, M.A. thesis, York University, Toronto, 1986.

MacGillivray, Allister, *The Cape Breton Fiddler*, College of Cape Breton Press, Sydney, N.S

Newlove, Harold J., *Fiddlers of the Canadian West*, Swift Current, 1976.

Ornstein, Lisa, A Life of Music : *History and Repertoire of Louis Boudreault, Traditional Fiddler from Chicoutimi*, M.A. thesis, Université de Laval, Quebec, 1985.

Proctor, George, "Old-Time Fiddling in Ontario", Anthropology Paper, National Museum, Ottawa, 1960.

Sellick, Lester B., *Canada's Don Messer*, Kentville, N.B., 1969.

Wechsberg, Joseph, *The Glory of the Violin*, Viking Press, N.Y., 1972.

The Canadian Folk Music Bulletin vol. 19, no. 3, September 1985 is devoted entirely to fiddling in Canada : Newfoundland (Neil Rosenberg), Cape Breton (Paul Cranford), N.S. (Bill Guest), P.E.I. (Jim Hornby), N.B. (Ivan Hicks), Sheenboro, Quebec (Christopher McGuire), Ontario (Anne Lederman), Kittley Township, Ontario (Elaine Keillor), Manitoba (Anne Lederman), The West (Jim Rogers), Pangnirtung, N.W.T. (John Bennett), Records (Richard Green), editor Anne Lederman.

Part II : Information on Fiddling

Amtmann, *Willi, La vie musicale dans la Nouvelle France*, Université de Strasbourg, 1956.

Anthology of Fiddle Styles, Mel Bay Publications.

Blaustein, Richard, *The Old Time Fiddlers' Association in the U.S.*, Ph.D. thesis, Indiana University, 1975.

Boyden, David, *The History of Violin Playing from its Origins to 1761*, Oxford University Press, London, 1965.

——"The Violin", *Musical Instruments Through the Ages*, Harmondsworth, Middlesex, Endland, 1963 & 1976.

Breathnach, Breandan, *Folk Music and Dance of Ireland*, Talbot Pres, Dublin, 1971.

Canadian Folk Music Bulletin.

The Cape Breton Fiddler, Newsletter of the Cape Breton Fiddler's Society

Cass-Beggs, Michael, *Folk Music and Dance of Ireland*, CBC, Montreal, 1971.

Collinson, Francis, *The Traditional and National Music of Scotland*, Routledge & Kegan Paul, London, 1966.

Cos, Gordon, *Folk Music in a Newfoundland Outpost*, Museum of Man, Mercury Series, Ottawa, 1980.

Country Music News, ed. Larry Delaney, Box 7323 Vanier Terminal, Ottawa, K1L 8E4 (numerous articles on Canadian fiddling, especially in *Fiddlers*

Corner by Bob Whitney, monthly, annual subscription $18.00

Coutre, Guillaume, *Tribute to Jean Carignan*, CBC, Montreal, 1973.

Desrosiers, *Roland, La Musique Traditionnelle au Québec*, Centre de documentation du Conseil Canadie des Arts populaires, Montreal, September, 1980.

Duncan, Craig, *Mel Bays Delux Fiddling Method*, 1981.

Dunlay, Kate, "A Cape Breton Primer", *Sing Out, The Folk Song Magazine*, vol. 34, no. 4, Fall, 1989.

Farmer, Henry, *A History of Music In Scotland*, Hinrichsen Edition, Ltd., London, 1947.

Folk-lore, L'Association québecoises des loisirs folkloriques, 4545 Ave. Pierre-de-Coubertin, Cassier postal 1000, Succursale M, Montreal. Complete information on fiddling in Quebec. Bi-monthly, annual subscription $12.00.

Gibbons, Roy, ed., *As It Comes : Folk Fiddling in Prince George*, B.C., Museum of Man, Mercury Series no. 42, Ottawa.

——*Folk Fiddling in Western Canada : A Sampling*, Museum of Man, Mercury Series no. 35, Ottawa, 1981.

——"La Grande Gigue simple and the Red River Jig", *Canadian Folk Music Journal*, vol. 8, 1980.

La Gigue, Le Centre de documentation du conseil canadian des arts populaires, Montreal, September, 1980.

Henebry, Richard, *A Handbook of Irish Music*, Cork University Press, Dublin, 1928.

Hogan, Dorthy & Homer, "Canadian Fiddle Culture", *Communique Canadian Studies*, 1977.

Hunter, James, *The Fiddle Music of Scotland*, W. Chambers, Edinburgh, 1979.

Johnson, David, *Music and Society in Lowland Scotland in the Eighteenth Century*, Oxford University Press, London, 1972.

Kallmann, Helmut, *A History of Music in Canada 1534-1914*, University of Toronto Press, Toronto, 1960.

Kaufman, Alan, *Beginning Old Time Fiddle*, Oak Publications, N.Y., 1977.

Kennedy, Norman John, *Growth and Development of Music in Canada*, University of Alberta, 1952.

Krassen, Miles, "An Analysis of a Jean Carignan Record", *Canadian Folk Music Journal*, vol. 2, 1974.

——*Appalachian Fiddle*, Oak Publications, N.Y., 1973

Malone, Bill C., *Country Music USA*, University of Texas Press, Austin, 1985.

Marcuse, Sybil, *Musical Instruction : a Comprehensive Dictionary*, Doubleday, Garden City, N.Y., 1964.

Moogk, Edward B., *Roll Back the Years : History of Canadian Record Sound and its Legacy*, National Library of Canada, Ottawa

Morrow, Mary, *Texas Fiddle Style*, University of Texas, Austin, 1980.

Old Time Music, 33 Brunswick Gardens, London, England.

O'Sullivan, Donal, *Irish Folk Music Song and Dance*, The Mercier Press, Cork, 1969.

Phillips, Stacy, *Bluegrass Fiddle Styles*, Oak Publications, 1978.

Russell, Kelly, *Rufus Guinchard : The Man and His Music*, St. John's, 1982.

Skinner, J. Scott, *The Scottish Violinist*, Bayley and Ferguson, Glasgow.

Spell, L., "Music in New France in the Seventeenth Century", *Canadian Historical Review*, vol. 8, no. 2.

Spielman, Earl V., "The Fiddling Traditions of Cape Breton and Texas : a Study in Parallels and Contrast". Yearbook for Inter-American Musical Research, vol. 8, 1972.

——*Traditional North American Fiddling : A Methodology*, Ph.D., thesis, University of Wisconsin, 1975.

Swackhammer, Macbeth, "I'm a Professional But I'm Not On Records", M.A. thesis, Memorial University, St. John's, 1979.

Thede, Marion Unger, *The Fiddle Book*, Oak Publications, N.Y., 1967.

Trudel, J., "La musique traditionnelle au Québec", *Possibles*, nos. 3-4, 1977.

Walter, Arnold, *Aspects of Music in Canada*, University of Toronto Press, Toronto, 1970.

Wolfe, Charles, Tennessee Strings, University of Tennessee Press, 1976.

Part III : Books of Fiddle Music

Allen, Ward, *Ward Allen Canadian Fiddle Tunes*, Book One, Toronto, BMI., 1956.

——Book Two, 1961.

Anthology of Jazz Violin, Mel Bay Publications, Pacific, Mo., U.S.A.

Avons, Adrien, *Reels et Jigs*, rev. ed., BMI, Toronto, 1961 (15 tunes).

Beaton, Donald Angus, *Cape Breton and Scottish Violin Music*.

Beaton, Joseph, *Mabou Music*, Casket Printing and Publishing Co. Ltd., Antigonish, N.S., 1980.

Beaton, Kinnon, *Beaton's Collection of Cape Breton Scottish Violin Music*, Port Hawkesbury, N.S., 1984.

——another book in preparation.

Begin, Carmelle, *Fiddle Music in the Ottawa Valley* (played by Dawson Girdwood), Museum of Man, Mercury Series no. 52, Ottawa, 1985.

Blues Fiddle, Mel Bay Publications.

Briand, Elmer, *The Elmer Briand Collection* (Mr. Briand is a Cape Breton Fiddler who lives in Halifax, N.S.)

Bruneau, Philippe, *La musique traditionnelle pour accordeon diatonique*, ed. Carmelle Begin, Museum of Man, Mercury Series no. 47, Ottawa, 1983 (70 tunes, 17 by Bruneau).

Carnaham, Gordie, *100 Toe Tappin' Tunes for Fiddle*, Hoedown Haven Publications, Brandon, Manitoba, 1989.

Christeson, R.P., *The Old Time Fiddler's Repertory*, University of Missouri Press, Columbia (245 tunes).

Cole, M.M., *One Thousand Fiddle Tunes*, M.M. Cole Publishing Co., Chicago, 1940.

Collector's Choice, *The Victorian Folk Music Club Incorporated*, Melbourne, Australia, vols 1 & 2 (500 fiddle tunes played in Australia).

Cormier, Bill, Cornhuskers Series no. 6, 44 original Canadian Jigs and Reels for Square Dance, Harry E. Jarman, Toronto.

The Cornhusker's Book of Old Time Fiddlin' Tunes, Harry E. Jarman, Toronto, 1938.

The Cornhusker's Book of Square Dance Tunes, Jarman Publications, Toronto, 1944.

Country Fiddling for Four Violins, Mel Bay Publications.

Daignault, Pierre, *En Place pour un set, trente parties de sets différents recueillis par Pierre Daignault*, Editions de l'Homme, Montreal, 1964.

Dawson, Peter, (book in preparation).

Dejarlis, Andy, *Andy Dejarlis Canadian Fiddle Tunes from the Red River Valley*, Book One, BMI, Toronto, 1958.

——Book Two, 1961.

——*Manitoba's Golden Fiddler*, BMI, Toronto, 1969.

Dewar, Malcolm, (book in preparation on music from Glengarry County, Ontario).

Dominion Round and Square Dances, Canadian Music Sales Co. Ltd., Toronto, 1956.

Dunlay, K.E. and D.L. Reich, *Traditional Celtic Fiddle Music of Cape Breton*, Fiddlecase Books, Peterborough, N.H.

E Z Way Fiddle Solos, Mel Bay Publications.

Fiddle Pocketbook, Mel Bay Publications.

The Fiddlecase Book of 101 Polkas, Fiddlecase Books, Peterborough, N.H.

The Fiddler's Fakebook, (500 tunes).

Folk Fiddle Styles, Mel Bay Publications.

Fourteen Fancy Fiddle Tunes, Mel Bay Publications.

Fraser, Simon, ed. *The Airs and Melodies Peculiar to The Highlands of Scotland and the Isles*, Edinburgh, 1816, reprinted by Paul Cranford, Sydney, N.S.

Ganam, King, *Canadian Fiddle Tunes*, BMI, Toronto, 1957.

Gibbons, Roy, *200 Old Time Fiddle Melodies from B.C.*, Canadian Centre for Folk Cultural Studies, ms., Ottawa, 1979.

Gillis, Wilf, (book in preparation).

Great Country Fiddle Solos, Mel Bay Publications.

Guest, Bill, *The Bill Guest Anthology of Fiddle Tunes*, Mel Bay Publications, 1985 (105 tunes).

——*A Hundred Fiddle Tunes in Down East Style*, Gordon V. Thompson, Ltd., Toronto, 1980.

——*Mel Bay's Delux Album of Fiddle Waltzes and Slow Airs*, Mel Bay Publications, 1988, (58 tunes).

——(several books in preparation).

Harding, Frank, *Harding's Collection of 200 Jigs, Reels and Country Dances*, Paul Pioneer Music Co., N.Y., 1928.

Haywood, Ernest and Newton, *Country Dances, Jigs, Reels and Strathspeys*, Keith Prowse Music Publishing Co. Ltd., London, 1924.

Hicks, Ivan, *Fiddle Tunes and Souvenirs*, Riverside, N.B., 1987, (29 tunes).

Irish Traditional Fiddle Music, Fiddlecase Books, Peterborough, N.H.

Issac, Burton, *Mel Bay's Bluegrass Fiddler*, Mel Bay Publications, 1974.

Joudrey, Robert, *Bluenose Facts and Fiddle Tunes*, Bridgewater, N.S. (15 tunes).

Joyce, Patrick, *Ancient Irish Music*, M.H. Gill and Son, Dublin, 1890.

Kennedy, Peter, *The Fiddler's Tune Book*, Harquail Music Press, N.Y., 1951.

——*The Second Fiddler's Tune Book*, 1954.

Kerr, James S., *Collection of Merry Melodies for the Violin*, 4 vols., Glasgow.

——*Kerr's First Collection of Merry Melodies for the Violin*, Glasgow, 1870.

——*Kerr's Second Collection…*, 1870.

——*Kerr's Third Collection…*, 1870.

——*Kerr's Collection of Reels, Strathspeys, Highland Schottishes, Country Dances, Hornpipes, Flirtations, etc.*, Glasgow.

Landry, Ned, *Bowing the Strings with Ned Landry*, Gordon V. Thompson, Toronto, 1959.

——*Ned Landry's Favorite Fiddle Tunes*, Emire Music, New Westminster, 1952.

Lunenburg County Fiddlers Club, Compositions by Lunenburg County Fiddlers, 1989.

MacDonald, Dan R., *The Heather Hill Collection*, ed. by John Donald Cameron, Brownrigg Publications, vol 1., (220 tunes).

MacDonald, Keith Norman, *Skye Collection of the Best Reels and Strathspeys*, Edinburgh, 1897, reprinted by Paul Cranford, Cape Breton, 1979.

MacEachern, Dan Hugh, *MacEachern's Collection of*

Cape Breton Scottish Music for the Violin, Queensville, N.S., 1975.

——(book in preparation).

McMillian, Roma, *Roma McMillan's Favorite Valley Waltzes*, OFC Publications, Ottawa, 1983, (75 tunes).

MacQuarrie, Gordon F. (arranged by), *The Cape Breton Collection of Scottish Melodies for the Violin*, J. Beaton, Medford, Mass., 1940, (151 tunes).

Magill, Jim, *Jim Magill's Square Dance Tunes*, Book One, for violin and piano, Jarman Publications, Toronto, 1950, 1952.

Marshall, William, *William Marshall's Scottish Melodies*, Fiddlecase Books, Peterborough, N.H.

Mel Bay's Old Time Fiddle Solos, 1977, (18 tunes).

Meredith, Mal, *Old Time Tunes*, Empire Music, New Westminster, 1954.

Messer, Don, *The Don Messer Anthology of Favorite Fiddle Tunes*, Gordon V. Thompson, Toronto, 1981, (190 tunes).

——*Don Messer's Barn Dance Breakdown*, Thompson, Toronto, 1954.

——*Don Messer's Canadian Hoedowns*, Thompson, Toronto, 1957.

——*Don Messer's Square Dance Tunes*, Canada Music Sales Corporation, Ltd., Toronto, 1952.

——*Don Messer's Way Down East Fiddlin' Tunes*, Thompson, Toronto, 1948.

——*Original Old Tyme Music*, Thompson, Toronto, 1942.

——*TV Favorites with Don Messer and His Islanders*, Canadian Music Sales Corporation, Toronto.

Miller, Randy and Jack Perron, *Irish Traditional Fiddle Music*, 3 vols. 1977.

New England Fiddler's Repertoire, Fiddlecase Books, Peterborough, N.H., 1983 (168 tunes).

One Hundred (100) Favorite Fiddle Solos, Mel Bay Publications.

O'Neill, Francis, *The Dance Music of Ireland : 1001 Gems*, Lyon and Healy, Chicago, 1907.

——*O'Neill's Music of Ireland : 1850 melodies*, Lyon and Healy, Chicago, 1903.

Petrie, George, *The Complete Collection of Irish Music*, London, 1905.

Phillips, Stacy, *Contest Fiddling*, Mel Bay Publications (33 tunes).

The Robbins Collection of 200 Jigs, Reels and Country Dances, United Artists Music, N.Y., 1933.

Roche, F., Collection of Irish Airs, Marches and Dance Tunes, 3 vols., Dublin, 1911.

Scott, Robert Samuel, *Canadian Fiddle Tunes*, BMI., Toronto, 1955.

Skinner, J. Scott, *The Scottish Violinist*, Bayley and Ferguson, Glasgow.

Smith, Gerry, *Canadian Fiddle Music*, Book 1, Riverside Music Publications, Exeter, Ontario, 1986, (22 tunes).

——*Presenting More Original Canadian Fiddle Music*, 1987, (25 tunes).

Smithwick, Cathy and Lynne, T*he Bluegrass Fiddle Songbook*, Charles Anderson Publishing, Melville, N.Y., 1980, (48 tunes).

Townsend, Graham, *Canadian Country Fiddle Tunes*, vol. 1, Berandol Music Ltd., Scarborough, 1971.

————Graham Townsend's *Canadian Fiddle Tunes*, Berandol.

——(book in preparation).

Vollrath, Calvin, (book in preparation).

Warhurst, Roy, (book in preparation).

White's Unique Collection of Jigs, Reels, etc., White-Smith Music, Chicago, 1902.

Williams, Vivian, ed., *151 Brand New Old Time Fiddle Tunes By Pacific Northwest Composers*, vol. 1, Voyager Publications, Seattle, 1983.

——*141 Brand New Old Time Fiddle Tunes*, vol. 2, 1986.

——*Pleasures at Home*, 1988.

Wilson, Derek, (book in preparation).

Discography

The original intention was to list every record or cassette containing Canadian fiddle music plus the names of the Canadian fiddle tunes and, under each tune in the book, the name of the records it was on. My own collection is over 100 records and a week's work in the National Library produced another 200 titles (2 copies of every book, record or cassette made in Canada should be sent to the National Library in Ottawa). Other sources turned up perhaps another 100 titles. That is a fraction of Canadian fiddle records, partly because so many records are locally produced. Listing them would fill a book, especially when fiddlers such as Townsend and Desjarlis have made around three dozen each. Tracking them all down would take a year and most are out of print.

So this discography lists 176 fiddlers or groups who have made records, and it is organized by province/region. Some fiddlers have been "moved around" : Wilf Gillis is listed with Cape Breton, Anne Lederman with Manitoba because that is appropriate for their music. Almost any fiddler in, say Manitoba, would know the 17 to 20 fiddlers there who have made records, and the ones in print will be on sale at competitions or in the stores that carry fiddle music. There are in addition a number of collections such as "Maple Sugar", or "Sixteen Great Fiddlers". Canadians have produced well over 500 records, probably 5000 tunes, 100 evenings of non-stop listening and that does not include 78s!

Newfoundland

Barron, Brian	Kitty Vitty Minstrels
Benoit, Emile	MacIssac, Walter
Guinchard, Rufus	Russell, Kelly
Hiscott, Richard	Snider, Jamie
Johnson, Roy	

Nova Scotia

Elliott, Carl	Joudrey, Robert
Elliott, Kirk	Mooring, Johnny
Guest, Bill	Ross, Keith
Higgins, Lorimer	Steele, Cye

Cape Breton

Beaton, Dan Angus	Chisholm, Angus
The Beatons of Mabou	Cormier, Joseph
Benoit Jarvis Quartet	Cremo, Leo
Boyd, Colin	Currie, Pat
Briand, Elmer	The Fiddlers of Cape
Campbell, John	Breton
The Cape Breton	Gillis, Alex
Symphony	Gillis, Wilfred
Chafe, Winnie	Glendale (annual record-

ing)
Fitzgerald, Winston "Scotty"
Holland, Jerry
Lamey, Bill
MacDonald, Dan R.
MacDonald, Howie
MacDonald, Jack
MacDougall, Mike

MacIntyr, Sandy
MacKenzie, Carl
MacKenzie, Hector
MacLean, Joe
MacLellan, Theresa
MacMaster, Natalie
MacPhee, Doug
Robichaud, Gerry

New Brunswick

Brogan, Mac
Chipman, Jimmy
Crawford, Winston
Hicks, Curtis
Hicks, Ivan
Jones, Crystal
Landry, Ned

Larocque, Etiene
LeBlanc, Elmo
Magee, Clayton
Messer, Don
Mitton, Earl
Murdoch, Matilda
Poirier, Eddy

Prince Edward Island

Arsenault, Alfred (Eddy)
Chaisson, Peter and Kenny
Chipman, Gary
MacDonald, Father Faber

MacIssac, Bill
Prince County Fiddlers
Prince Edward Island Fiddlers

Quebec

Alain, André
Allard, Joseph
Boudreault, Louis
Bujeau, Théo
Carignan, Jean
Croisetiére, Roland
Cuillerier, Yvon
Cyr, Clément
Dinelle, Raymond
Gagnier, Guy
Gagnon, André
Girard, Rosaire
Godin, André
Guérette, Gilbert
Labbe, Gabriel
Labrecque, Jacques
Lacroix, Henri

Landry, Charlie
Landry, Henri
Landry, Pierre Antoine
Laplante, Rosaire
Lavoie, Isadore
Lecours, Marcel
Les Fréres Lizotte
Montmarquette, Alfred
Ornstein, Lisa
Pointu, Monsieur
Poliquin, Raymond
Richard, Ti-Blanc
Rioux, Therese
Soucy, Isidore
La Turlutaine
Vallée, Bob
Verette, Jean-Marie

Ottawa Valley

Allen, Jim
Allen, Ward
Brisson, Denis
Conners, Jim
Curry, Nathan
The Dagenais Family

Hebert, Brian
Hill, Reg
Lalonde, Bobby
Lanctôt, Denis
McMillan, Roma
Mostly Bows

Dawson, Peter
Glengarry Strathspey and Reel Society
Hayes, Howard

Ranger, Bob
Renfrew County Fiddlers
Trottier, Kelly
Whitney, Bob

Ontario

Adlam, Claire
Andrews, Abbie
Arbuckle, Bob
Bates, Smiley
Brown, Bobby
Burtnik, Tony
Cherny, Al
The Cornhuskers
Currie, Pat
Eikhard, June
Givens, Johnny
Gyurki, Ed
Harrison, Joe
Irving, Bill
Joyce, Chuck

Kishuk, Pete
The Leahy Family
MacNaughton, Karl
Meeks, Rudy
Menard, Paul
Morrison, Randy
Muddy York
Pasowisty, Vic
The Shryer Triplets
Smith, Gerry
Townsend, Eleanor
Townsend, Graham
Wade, George
Woods, Scott

Manitoba

Bedard, Mel
Brown, Johnny
Bouvette, Reg
Carnahan, Gordie
Cherneckie, Cam
Dejarlis, Andy
Forman, Barry
Kusturok, Patti
Laderoute, Eugene

Lamb, Grant
Lederman, Anne
Machan, Walter
Meilleur, Marcel
Mrozik, Ron
Muirhead, Sam
Plohman, Crystal
Wright, Harold

Saskatchewan

Grand Coulee Old Tyme Jug Band
Ganam, King
Magill, Jim
Maple Creek Old Tyme Fiddlers

Swift Current Old Time Fiddlers
Town and Country Orchestra (Esterhazy)

Alberta

Calgary Fiddlers
Foggy River Band
Myhre, Alfie
Ron Paxton and the Foothill Stompers

Udale, Elmer
Vollrath, Calvin
Warhurst, Roy

British Columbia

Barron, Myllie
Ferrel, Frank
Hanley Old Time Fiddlers

Kienlein, Kevin
Rodgers, Frankie

Record Companies and Distributors

Dozens of companies make records and many have small studios which come and go or move around. The best way to get records is to contact the fiddlers–Graham Townsend, for example, has been recorded on numerous labels. The best source is the catalogue from the Canadian Society for Musical Traditions, CSMT Mail Order Service, 213, 2723-37th Avenue, N.E., Calgary, T1Y 5R8. Here are a few important distributors, not including the companies of individual fiddlers such as Ivan Hicks or Ray Warhurst.

Boot Records, 1343 Matheson Blvd. E, Missassauga, Ontario, L4W 1R1

Brownrigg Productions, 37 Nottawasaga Cres, Brampton, Ontario, L6Z 1B8

Camden (RCA), Pickwick Records, 106-108 McMaster, Ajax, Ontario, L1S 2E7

Canadian Folk Music Society, Box 4232, Calgary, Alberta, T2T 5N1

Celtic (London), 6265 Cote de Liesse, St. Laurent, Quebec, H4T 1C3

Cranford, Paul, Box 42, Englishtown, Cape Breton, N.S., B0C 1H0

Goodtyme Productions, 202-1280 Archibald Street, Winnipeg, Manitoba, R2J 0Z3

Hillcan Sales, 1145 Bellamy Road N., Unit 13-14, Scarborough, Ontario, M1H 1H5

Holborne Records, (Celtic, Rodeo, Banff), 510 Coronation Drive, Unit 17, West Hill, Ontario, M1E 4X6

MCA Coral, 2450 Victoria Park Avenue, Willowdale, Ontario, M2J 4A2

Pigeon Inlet Productions (Kelly Russell), Site 13, Box 26, R.R. 1, Torbay, Newfoundland, A0A 3Z0

Rounder Records, 186 Willow Avenue, Sommerville, Massachussetts, USA, 02144

Sunflower Records, 22 Flora Avenue, Winnipeg, Manitoba, R2W 2P8

Sunshine Records, 228 Selkirk Avenue, Winnipeg, Manitoba, R2W 2L6

University College of Cape Breton Press, Box 5300, Sydney, N.S., B1P 6L2

Voyager Recordings (Vivian Williams), 424-35th Avenue, Seattle, Washington, USA, 98122

Diana, Ed, Kai, Denise Whitcomb
Irish Ambassador's National Day Reception, March 17, 2000
New Delhi, India.

But hornpipes, jigs, strathspeys and reels
Put life and mettle in their heels.

Robbie Burns

His elbows all were greased with gin
And his heart and soul were warmed within;
He picked up the fiddle and the bow he drew
And the dancers like chained lightening flew.

Larry Gorman, PEI

For the good are always the merry,
Save by an evil chance,
And the merry love the fiddle
And the merry love to dance.